Rapture Ready

GET RIGHT OR GET LEFT

JAMES H. RAYNER

authorHOUSE®

AuthorHouse™
1663 Liberty Drive
Bloomington, IN 47403
www.authorhouse.com
Phone: 1 (800) 839-8640

Scripture quotations marked KJV are from the Holy Bible, King James Version (Authorized Version). First published in 1611. Quoted from the KJV Classic Reference Bible, Copyright © 1983 by The Zondervan Corporation.

Scripture quotations marked NKJV are taken from the New King James Version. Copyright © 1982 by Thomas Nelson, Inc. Used by permission. All rights reserved.

Published by AuthorHouse 07/26/2016

ISBN: 978-1-5246-1857-5 (sc)
ISBN: 978-1-5246-1855-1 (hc)
ISBN: 978-1-5246-1856-8 (e)

Library of Congress Control Number: 2016911342

ACKNOWLEDGMENT

I would like to acknowledge my wife Kathi, who has been my pillar in the ministry all these years, and my daughter Natalie, along with her husband Ivan, for my first grandson; Antonio James, to be delivered into this world in my birth month of August, 2016.

For Antonio:

1 Peter 2:9 But you are *a chosen generation, a royal priesthood, a holy nation, His own special people, that you may proclaim the praises of Him who called you out of darkness into His marvelous light;*

This book is dedicated to:
Yeshua; *The Bridegroom,*
Our Blessed Hope
We await your return

INTRODUCTION

This book is not just an easy read, although it may be easy to read. This book is set up to get the proper Scriptures in your spirit. This book is set up so that you may know beyond a shadow of a doubt what you must do to get rapture ready. The Scriptures are Precept upon precept and line upon line, and given in such a way as to give you an understanding of the rapture. I have rightly divided the word of truth without infringing upon the authority of my Lord and Savior Jesus Christ, or the Father in heaven who has put the time of the rapture in his authority. In a day and age when many want to make a name for themselves by knowing when the rapture is coming, and when the tribulation is coming; I dare not try to convince you of pre-tribulation, mid-tribulation, or post-tribulation ideology. I'm merely presenting the prophetic Scriptures as given to me by the Holy Ghost. I want you to know I will be repeating Scriptures. Sometimes I will say the same thing over again, but other times it will be in reference to a totally different idea, and as I said before it's for the purpose of giving you a hope, helping you to adorn yourself, and getting you rapture ready. Regardless of what anyone says doctrinally God gave me these words to tell you. **Get Right or Get Left.**

Your Friend,
James H. Rayner

WHO

In this particular segment we must determine who is going to inherit the kingdom of God. We will do this by first determining who is not going to inherit the kingdom of God. This decision is ultimately in God's hands. We are using qualifiers in the word of God to do what every teacher of the gospel should be doing.

JEWISH CUSTOMS

In the Jewish marriage customs a young man chooses the bride. He then negotiates with her father that they may be betrothed. The young man presents three things to the father, a dowry, a contract, and a cup of wine. The young lady is called forth, and if she approves and drinks of the cup of wine, the covenant is ratified. She is betrothed and to be married. The young man returns home to his father, where he begins to build onto the family home. Once he is finished building, and once the father is satisfied with his effort and timing he tells the son to go get his bride and bring her to the home.

THE RAPTURE IS IN THE FATHERS HANDS
AN EXCEEDINGLY GREAT OPERATION

This operation having been put in the hands of the Almighty father must be of extreme importance because we know that he framed the worlds and he set the ornaments in space, and of these projects were no short-term task. The following Scripture says who hath measured the waters in the hollow of his hand, and meted out the heaven with us with the span, and comprehended the dust of the earth in a measure and weighed the mountains in scales and the Hills in a balance. This is God. Do you wonder how big God is? He is a great big God, and telling his son to go for the bride is a great big project.

GOD ADORNED THE KOSMOS

Isaiah 40:12 (KJV) Who hath measured the waters in the hollow of his hand, and meted out heaven with the span, and comprehended the dust of the earth in a measure, and weighed the mountains in scales, and the hills in a balance?

HOW BIG IS GOD?

For those of you who asked the question how big is God, well I can tell you he measured the waters of the earth in the hollow of his hand. That looks to me like a great big God. The word says he comprehended the dust of the earth in a measure. That looks like a great big God, and he weighed the mountains in a scale. Where do you think he got the scale to weigh the mountains?

God is a great big God. The word of God says that he's exceedingly great.

JESUS IS COMING FOR HIS BRIDE

John 14:2-3 (KJV)
In my Father's house are many mansions: if *it were* not *so*, I would have told you. I go to prepare a place for you. 3 And if I go and prepare a place for you, I will come again, and receive you unto myself; that where I am, *there* ye may be also.

Abraham sends for Isaacs bride

She must be of his kinsman
Gen 24 *Let's take a look at Isaacs bride which is a type of Christ's Bride (the church)*
FATHER ABRAHAM*: sent his servant Eliezer to Mesopotamia; the place where his kindred dwells because he did not want his son to marry from the Canaanites, but from his kindred.*

ELIEZER THE SERVANT: *Eliezer goes to Mesopotamia to bring back a bride for Abraham's son. His intention is to bring back a bride of Abraham and Isaac's kindred.*

Eliezer makes a decree that sets a standard for the particular person, who is to be the bride? Rebecca meets the standard because she yields to the demands of Eliezer and shows that she is a person's zealous of good works. Eliezer gives Rebecca gifts. Rebecca leaves her family and gladly goes with him to be married to Isaac. As far as the family and the other young women who met at the well at this time, many are called but few are chosen. The other women were not of the family, nor did they meet the standards of the decree.

ISAAC: *Isaac awaits his bride. Rebecca takes the journey back to Haran where Abraham and Isaac dwell. When Rebecca arrives she asked Eliezer who is that one in the field. He responds that is Isaac. At that time she lit off the camel, and ran to Isaac, for she had said unto the servant, what man is this that walketh in the field to meet us? And the servant had said it is my master: therefore she had taken a vail, and covered herself.*

Rebecca:

A PEOPLE ZEALOUS OF GOOD WORKS
Titus 2:13-14 (KJV) **reference scripture**

Rebecca, the bride of Isaac; was zealous of good works. She yielded
To Eliezer and refreshed him with water. She also watered the camels. (A camel can drink 30 gallons of water, and there were 10 camels). She was familiar with working hard and showed great hospitality.

Jesus gave himself for us to purify us and make us a holy people and a people that are zealous of good works just like Rebecca. If Rebecca can be as committed as she was for Isaac how can we do any less for our Lord who gave himself for us.

On Rebecca's journey to Isaac, once he is viewed, she lit off of the camel and ran to him.

Participants of the rapture:

God the father, God the son, God the Holy Spirit, the church (the bride) When Jesus is in view our blessed Hope is one of a desire to embrace with the bone we will spend all eternity with.

JESUS IS TRULY OUR BLESSED HOPE.

GODS PERSPECTIVE

FATHER GOD SENT THE SON TO RECEIVE A KINGDOM
Sent to receive what is very valuable to God the father

Luke 19:12 (KJV)
He said therefore, a certain nobleman went into a far country to receive for himself a kingdom, and to return.

This was Jesus' first coming. He came as a nobleman into a far country to receive a kingdom and return. As he went into the city and the people said hosanna they were receiving the kingdom, but shortly thereafter they killed him rejecting the king

JESUS

Matt 13:44-48 (KJV)

Again, the kingdom of heaven is like unto treasure hid in a field; the which when a man hath found, he hideth, and for joy thereof goeth and selleth all that he hath, and buyeth that field. Again, the kingdom of heaven is like unto a merchant man, seeking goodly pearls: Who, when he had found one pearl of great price, went and sold all that he had, and bought it. Again, the kingdom of heaven is like unto a net, that was cast into the sea, and gathered of every kind: Which, when it was full, they drew to shore, and sat down, and gathered the good into vessels, but cast the bad away.

The treasure in the field is the church.
The one who sold all that he had and bought the field was Jesus
the merchant man seeking goodly pearls was Jesus
he found one of great price, which is the church he sold all that he had and bought it
Jesus is also the one who cast the net, and when it was full he with joy cast out the bad, and gathered the good ones into the vessel.

John 14:15-17 If ye love me, keep my commandments. And I will pray the Father, and he shall give you another Comforter, that he may abide with you for ever; *Even* the Spirit of truth; whom the world cannot receive, because it seeth him not, neither knoweth him: but ye know him; for he dwelleth with you, and shall be in you.

Jesus said in my father's house are many mansions if it were not true I would've told you. He says: I will go and prepare a place for you, that I may receive you unto myself, that where I am you may be also

It is God the father who will give the command for the son to come to the earth, and received his bride.

THE HOLY SPIRIT

John 16:13-14 (KJV)
Howbeit when he, the Spirit of truth, is come, he will guide you into all truth: for he shall not speak of himself; but whatsoever he shall hear, *that* shall he speak: and he will shew you things to come. He shall glorify me: for he shall receive of mine, and shall shew *it* unto you.

Jesus loves you

Eph 5:25-27 (KJV)
Husbands, love your wives, even as Christ also loved the church, and gave himself for it; That he might sanctify and cleanse it with the washing of water by the word, That he might present it to himself a glorious church, not having spot, or wrinkle, or any such thing; but that it should be holy and without blemish

There is a Standard to enter the kingdom of heaven

Eph 5:5 For this ye know, that no whoremonger, nor unclean person, nor covetous man, who is an idolater, hath any inheritance in the kingdom of Christ and of God.

Romans 6:19 I speak after the manner of men because of the infirmity of your flesh: for as ye have yielded your members servants to uncleanness and to iniquity unto iniquity; even so now yield your members servants to righteousness unto holiness

We will be matured in the earth, and then transformed, ready for heaven

JESUS: *Just as Rebecca lit off of the camel to meet Isaac so shall the bride of Christ be raptured to meet Jesus in the air.*

We must mature in God

Eph 4:13-14 (KJV)
The word of God's is that we will come into the unity of faith and of the knowledge of the son of God, unto a perfect man and to the measure of the stature of the fullness of Christ. In other words we will be matured in the things of God, no more like children tossed to and fro and carried about with every wind of doctrine by the slightest of Manning cunning craftiness

whereby we lie in wait to be deceived. In other words we will grow up, walking in the fullness of God. We shall be conformed to the image of Christ, not being deceived by the devil, not being deceived by preachers, not being deceived by the world, and walking in the full stature of Christ.

PERFECT= *Teleious / Growth in mental, and moral character. Mature in the things of God*

We will be transformed to be like him

1 John 3:2-3 (KJV)
There is to be a transformation when Jesus appears we will be transformed to be like Jesus those who are watching and praying and waiting. We don't even know what he will change us to, but we know that we will be like him. This promises to everyone who hopes and rejoice in his appearing, for we will be pure as he is pure

Who aspires to go in the rapture?
What are the qualifications needed
First and foremost you must be born again

This is a good start

John 3:3 (KJV)
Jesus answered and said unto him, Verily, verily, I say unto thee, except a man be born again, he cannot see the kingdom of God.
I believe that the rapture is for the bride out of the church.

This Scripture does not say that everyone is going in the rapture, even though he has a mansion for you

John 14:1-3 (KJV) In my Father's house are many mansions: if *it were* not *so*, I would have told you. I go to prepare a place for you. And if

I go and prepare a place for you, I will come again, and receive you unto myself; that where I am, *there* ye may be also.

Watch and pray that you may escape

Luke 21:36 (KJV)
Watch ye therefore, and pray always, that ye may be accounted worthy to escape all these things that shall come to pass, and to stand before the Son of man.

I believe that these things that we are to escape, that shall come to pass are the things that will take place during the tribulation.

Jesus is our blessed hope

Titus 2:13-14 (KJV)
This Scripture says that we are looking for the blessed hope, and the glorious appearing of the great God and our Savior Jesus Christ. That can mean nothing but the rapture. That can mean nothing but the appearing of **Jesus which is our blessed hope.** It also says that he gave himself for us that we might be redeem from all iniquity. The realize it is iniquity that keeps us from getting in heaven. It's sin that keeps us from getting in heaven. The only way the whole church can be the bride is that all would be purified when Jesus returns, because of the hope of his return. I ask you the question is all of the church hoping for his return? Is all of the church believing that he will return? Does all of the church have the doctrine and is being taught about his return? The answer has to be no. The word of God says in 1 John 3:2 – 3 that when he appears we will see him as he is, and we will be like him. Every one that has this hope will be purified as he is pure. This is what will prepare us for the transformation that we may be fit for heaven. **He also says he gave himself for us that we might be redeem from sin and iniquity, that he may purify unto himself a peculiar people, zealous of good works.** This purification

may take place when Jesus returns, but until then we are a peculiar people, designated to be to be zealous of good works.

Zealous of good works FEAR GOD FOR HE, AND HE ONLY DETERMINE WHO GOES TO HEAVEN

Luke 12:4-5 (KJV) But I will forewarn you whom ye shall fear: Fear him, which after he hath killed hath power to cast into hell; yea, I say unto you, Fear him.

Though we are not told who is going in the rapture, we are told some of the guidelines that will get us there, and that will get us to heaven. We are also told what will hinder us from getting there. By no means am I trying to determine who is going and who is not but I will do like every preacher does on Sunday or the Sabbath and rather than place one in heaven or hell I will do what it says in Ephesians 4 and do my best to equip the saints.

Eph 4:13-14 (KJV)

Till we all come in the unity of the faith, and of the knowledge of the Son of God, unto a perfect man, unto the measure of the stature of the fulness of Christ: **14** That we *henceforth* be no more children, tossed to and fro, and carried about with every wind of doctrine, by the sleight of men, *and* cunning craftiness, whereby they lie in wait to deceive;

> *Until the father actually says to Jesus; son go get your bride, what I am presenting to you is instruction as written in the word of God.*

As a student of the Bible it is your job to rightly divide the word of truth. I will present the word of God that was given to me through the anointing of the Holy Spirit, and your job is to hear, research and see if it's true, and supply the faith if it is.

I would not dare attempt to undermine the authority of God and say who is to go in the rapture, but God has given me a strong indication through parables and metaphors and scriptures for instruction, and they cannot be received any other way. I present them to you. Truly in the old testament is the new testament concealed, and in the New Testament is the old testament revealed. In the Old Testament is the new testament contained, and in the new testament is the old testament explained.

THE GOOD NEWS IS THAT WE HAVE A HOPE AND EXPECTATION BECAUSE OF THE WORD OF GOD.

We are not told to guess when the rapture is to take place, but __we are told to watch and pray that we may escape the trial or tribulation that is coming upon the earth.__

Based on the sequence of the truth and the word of God, we can discern the season and the time without expecting to know the exact day or hour.

Blotted out of the book of life

Psalms 69:26-29 (KJV)
For they persecute *him* whom thou hast smitten; and they talk to the grief of those whom thou hast wounded. Add iniquity unto their iniquity: and let them not come into thy righteousness. Let them be blotted out of the book of the living, and not be written with the righteous.

Remember to repent
because your works are not perfect

Rev 3:1-4 (KJV)
<u>Repent of these things and watch for my coming, or be blotted out of the book of life.</u>

The Scripture says that you appeared to be living, but you are ready to die **because your works are not perfect before God. You must repent you must remember how you received the word before and how you helped pass before and repent.** And if you don't watch I will come on the as a thief and you shall not know the hour that I come.

You can be blotted out you must overcome

Rev 3:4-6 (KJV)
He that overcometh, the same shall be clothed in white raiment**; and I will not blot out his name out of the book of life,** but I will confess his name before my Father, and before his angels.

He that hath an ear, let him hear what the Spirit saith unto the churches.

You shall overcome

This is the church of Sardis who has a reputation for being a living church, not lukewarm, not hypocritical, but they have a reputation and appearance for being a living church but the Lord says that they are close to death, he says to repent and remember how you received the word before. This proves that the word of God is faith food, and only the faithful can overcome. The Lord tells them to overcome, and they shall be clothed in white raiment; and I will not blot your name out of the book of life, but I will confess your name before my father, and before his Angels. He that have an ear, let him hear what the Spirit says unto the churches.

WE ARE CHILDREN OF THE LIGHT

1 Thess 5:4-7 (KJV) But ye, brethren, are not in darkness, that that day should overtake you as a thief. 5 Ye are all the children of light, and the children of the day: we are not of the night, nor of darkness.

Because we are children of the light, that day will not overtake us. God gives us an urgency in our spirits to prepare for the coming of Christ.

Because we truly love him we cannot help but to attend to keeping oil in our lamps, and trimming our wick.

WE ARE SOBER AND NOT ASLEEP

6 Therefore let us not sleep, as do others; but let us watch and be sober. 7 For they that sleep, sleep in the night; and they that be drunken are drunken in the night.

When is the rapture going to take place?
Pre-tribulation, mid-tribulation, or post-tribulation.
It is not for you to know the times or the seasons, which the Father hath put in his own power.
Power = Exousia in the Greek which means authority.
Stop violating God the father's authority.

We have thousands of ministers trying to tell us when.
What does God say about in his word?
It's time we begin to say what God has placed in his word.

Acts 1:6-7 (KJV) And he said unto them, It is not for you to know the times or the seasons, which the Father hath put in his own power.

It is not for you to know the times or the seasons, which the Father hath put in his own power.
It is not for you to know.

Ultimately the rapture is when God says it is.
God the father is showing his role as the father of the bridegroom.

His plan is for his son to come to the earth and get his bride for the marriage supper of the Lamb, while the wrath of God, (tribulation), is taking place on the earth. The word of God says that God has not designed us for wrath. This means that the tribulation is not for us, but if we neglect this great salvation, how shall we escape the tribulation.

Heb 2:2-3 (KJV) How shall we escape, if we neglect so great salvation;
this Scripture is letting us know that there is some escape but in order to acquire this escape we must not neglect our salvation. We must attend the things that are in the word of God and will allow us to escape the tribulation which is about to come upon the whole earth.

WE MUST GET TO KNOW HIM

to know him is to love him
Matt 7:21-23 (KJV) Not every one that saith unto me, Lord, Lord, shall enter into the kingdom of heaven; but he that doeth the will of my Father which is in heaven. 22 Many will say to me in that day, Lord, Lord, have we not prophesied in thy name? and in thy name have cast out devils? and in thy name done many wonderful works? 23 And then will I profess unto them, I never knew you: depart from me, ye that work iniquity.

Mark 13:31-32 (KJV) But of that day and that hour knoweth no man, no, not the angels which are in heaven, neither the Son, <u>but the Father.</u>

WHO IS TO GO IN THE RAPTURE?

*The final say belongs to the Father, but we have been given some qualifiers that can put us more at eased.

<u>*We can look at the blessed hope, and hope; and not look at the tribulation in fear.*</u>

Since I first heard and understood the rapture, I've had a hope of going to heaven this way. I periodically caught things in the Scripture that later turned out to be what I now know our qualifications for going in the rapture.

These Scriptures gave me an innate sense of the difference between a qualified Christian and one who is neglecting his salvation.

Heb 2:3 How shall we escape, if we neglect so great salvation;

SALVATION FROM THE TRIAL

We have more than one salvation of which the rapture is one.
Our main salvation is when Jesus saved us from sin and death and re-created our spirits unto righteousness.
The rapture is the salvation by which we are saved from the wrath of God.

BOTTOM LINE-WE MUST PLEASE GOD

*Who aspires to be raptured?, and what are the qualifiers as we see them?

WATCHING AND PRAYING

Luke 21:36 (KJV) Watch ye therefore, and pray always, that ye may be accounted worthy to escape all these things that shall come to pass, and to stand before the Son of man.

BE ACCOUNTED WORTHY TO ESCAPE

Watching and praying may qualify you to be accounted worthy to escape these things that shall come to pass.

We must understand that one of the jobs of the Holy Spirit as teacher is to prepare you that you may go in the rapture. You must understand that the barley is the grain of the Lord, and this grain must be separated from the chaff or sin by the winnowing of the Holy Spirit which blows away the chaff or sin from the barley. The wheat is also a grain which is waived before the Lord, but it has a harder shell which must be crushed to be prepared for harvest.

You as a Christian can determine whether you are to be winnowed because of the tenderness of your heart towards the Lord which will allow you to discard sin with the teaching and application of the word of God taught by the Holy Spirit, or you can be rebellious and in different to the word of God allowing a hard heart to keep you from the love of God. If you lost your first love get to know him again. Don't wait too late because you may have to be crushed in order to discard the sins or the chaff of the wheat.

Yielding to the wind (Holy Spirit)

The word spirit, and the word wind are the same word in Hebrew.

Which are you? Are you preparing by the Holy Spirit to be harvested in the rapture by yielding to the wind (Holy Spirit). Or are you going to wait till the end, and then dedicate in preparation for heaven.

Lord; I want to be ready. Holy Spirit please prepare me so that I may go in the rapture. I want to be accounted worthy to escape the trial that is to come upon the whole earth.

BEING OBEDIENT TO GOD

Rev 3:10 (KJV)
Because thou hast kept the word of my patience, I also will keep thee from the hour of temptation, which shall come upon all the world, to try them that dwell upon the earth.

*This Scripture is showing that there are two qualifiers that God honors and will keep his people from the hour of temptation that is to come upon the whole world, which I believe to be the tribulation. These two qualifiers that will keep his people from going to the tribulation is **keeping his word of patience.***

THIS HOPE PURIFIES

1 John 3:1- 3 (KJV) 2 Beloved, now are we the sons of God, and it doth not yet appear what we shall be: but we know that, when he shall appear, we shall be like him; for we shall see him as he is. **3 And every man that hath this hope in him purifieth himself, even as he is pure**

*God also says that Jesus gave himself for us that he may redeem us from iniquity and purify us unto himself **a peculiar people, zealous of good works.***

Having the blessed hope

Speaking to those who are to go in the rapture 1 John 3:1- 3 says that we do not know what we will become, but we do know that we will be like

Jesus when he appears, and one of the purifying factors is hope. This hope will purify us to be purified even as Jesus is purify which means holy.

Because sin cannot enter heaven we must be changed before we get there. So there must be a hope which purifies us and prepares us for a change.

WE HAVE A HOPE

Zealous of good works

*So another qualifier would be a people who conform to his original reason for redemption which is that we may become a peculiar people and **that we might be zealous of good works.***

Let us look at the 10 virgins five foolish and five wise

To trim, or to adorn oneself
7 Then all those virgins arose, and trimmed their lamps.

Matt 25:1-13 (KJV) What makes the five wise virgins wise. We also spoke of being zealous of good works. Where are the good works. If these wise virgins were to go with the bridegroom where are the good works. I personally believe that the good works are shown in Matthew 25:7. Here it says that the virgins arose and trimmed their lamps. The word trim here means to attend to or to adorn. **I believe the bride of Christ is to become wise by adorning herself with the word of God**. I believe the main factor was attending to the word of God. The Bible says, thy word is a lamp unto my feet, and a light unto my path so the word of God gives us an illumination or light. But you cannot have illumination without the anointing, which is the oil of the Holy Spirit. You cannot have the illumination fully if you don't trim the wick. Trimming the wick is one of the words for adorning or adorning the wick. If we adorn ourselves we are trimming the wick and allowing the word of God to flow forth unhinered. The word adorn means to arrange one's self in an orderly fashion.

PUT OFF, PUT ON

Eph 4:22-24 (KJV)

That ye put off concerning the former conversation the old man, which is corrupt according to the deceitful lusts; And be renewed in the spirit of your mind; And that ye put on the new man, which after God is created in righteousness and true holiness.

This the Scripture is saying put off that old man who is corrupt and lustful and follows his flesh or body in the corrupt appetites more than his new renewed spirit. Since we have been renewed in the spirit of our mind, we are a new creature and called a new man. It also implies that we are created in righteousness and true holiness, and because of this we must walk in the path of the new man. Put off the old corrupt man put on the new righteous man..

James 1:21 (KJV) says and that we must lay aside all filthiness and superfluity of naughtiness, and receive with meekness the engrafted word which is able to save our soul. Which means that to engraft or make the word of God a part of our soul which is our thoughts will and emotions that once we have stepped into eternity these parts of our soul will be saved.

<u>WE ARE THE CHILDREN OF THE LIGHT, SO WE MUST</u>

WATCH AND PRAY

YIELD TO THE HOLY SPIRIT

BE OBEDIENT TO GOD

HAVE THE BLESSED HOPE

BE ZEALOUS OF GOOD WORKS

PUT OFF, PUT ON

Do the best you can do

*I am not saying that the aforementioned qualifications are the only qualifications, nor am I saying that we must attain to all, because the ultimate decision is in the hands of the father. I'm not saying that our salvation is not sure either, because the word of God says that the Holy Ghost is our guarantee or as is put in the Scriptures; an earnest of the promise.

Being a part of God's great harvest

*Below I have put together an overview of the feast of Israel. This overview is not to show the feast themselves but merely the rapture Saints, the tribulation Saints, and the grapes of wrath. Showing the feasts of Israel is merely showing where each of these events are to occur. **Pay particular attention to the barley harvest, the wheat harvests, and the grapes of wrath.***

FEAST OF PASSOVER

FEAST OF UNLEAVEN BREAD

FEAST OF FIRST FRUITS -

THE BARLEY HARVEST - WINNOWED BY WIND

TINDER AND OBEDIENT

At the time of barley harvest, the priest would go out into the barley field and take a handful of barley offering it up unto the Lord and then taking the handful of barley to the Temple. He would then offer a sacrifice, a lamb.

This action would render the whole field of barley sanctified.

The significance of this harvest appears to relate to the harvest of the saints.

First of all barley is a very tender crop. It cannot be bruised. The way that it is harvested is by winnowing. As the barley is winnowed it is tossed to the sky and then caught. This process causes chaff to be separated by the wind. The word wind is the same word is spirit in Hebrew. The word Ruach. This shows that the Holy Spirit has everything to do with the processing of the first harvests. This harvest was processed preferably at night when the wind was right.

FEAST OF PENTECOST

WHEAT HARVEST THE WHEAT IS HARD
MUST BE CRUSHED- SAVED, BUT LITTLE REGARD FOR THE WORD of God

The wheat harvest was processed after the feast of Pentecost. The process was different from the harvesting of the barley. Wheat is a harder grain and the must be crushed in order to separate the chaff from the wheat. The process goes as such. The wheat is laid on the ground and covered with a board. The board is attached to a mule by rope. The mule goes forward and crushes the wheat. The name of the board that is used to crush the wheat is called a tribulon (reminds you of the tribulation doesn't it).

It appears as though some of the Christians that have an opportunity to be winnowed won't, but will wait for the tribulation unaware that these trials will crush.

FEAST OF TRUMPETS

LET ME EXPLAIN

THE BARLEY HARVEST (THE RAPTURE SAINTS)
THOSE WHO OBEY AND HIGHLY REGARD THE WORD

I've shown you the barley harvests and those who are sitting under the word of God and trying with all they have to attain to the life of God, and who are looking for the blessed hope and Jesus's return. They allow the Holy Spirit to blow away the chaff or sin in their life, as they fellowship with the Lord.

1 Thess 3:12-13 (NKJV)

All of the Scripture can be shown in one word, and that word is love.

In this passage of Scripture 1 Thess 3:12–13 Paul is saying here that his desire for Thessalonica is that they may abound in love towards each other and he desires that they may be blameless so that they may go in the rapture when the Lord appears. It is a benefit for your heart to be established in for you to be blameless and pure in holiness when Jesus arrives.

We must continue to sit before the Lord received the word of God and allow the Holy Spirit to establish us that we may be blameless before the Lord when he arrives that we may be before him without spot and without wrinkle. Jesus said that's the type of church he's coming for, the one without spot and without wrinkle. And he will bring those with him who have passed on before.

1 Thess 4:16-18 (NKJV)

The Scripture expresses the character of Jesus's return. We look for the Lord shout, we look for the voice of an Archangel, and we look for the trumpet of God, and then the dead in Christ shall rise, and we who remain will be caught up. We'll wait for the dead in Christ to rise first and then the grand finale of all. Something that has never happened in all of history; we shall be changed to be like him, and caught up to meet him in the air.

What a glorious grand finale that will be. We are also told the comfort one another with these words. Truly the greatest comfort you can give anyone is to let them know that they will see their relatives that have that have die once again they will receive their friends who left this earth most people will be looking forward to seeing their mother and father again. I'm quite sure this is the greatest hope of anyone other than seeing Jesus himself who made it all possible.

Paul is saying here in 2 Thess 1:3–12 (NKJV that Everlasting punishment comes to those who do not know the Lord, and to those who do not obey his word, and to those who trouble the people of Thessalonica. Paul is saying that he boast on these Christians of Thessalonica for what they've gone through to be established in Christ.

This is not showing cruelty when God's gives everlasting punishment to those who do not know him. This is not saying to those who were not offered Christ, but to those who refused him and did not get to the second stage which is having an intimate relationship with him.

THE WHEAT HARVEST (TRIBULATION SAINTS)

Then I've shown you the wheat harvests in those Christians who may have received Christ as their Savior but have no interest in Jesus at all. They are Christians in name only. All they go to church and most times for entertainment or something to do but they have no personal relationship with Jesus and they don't allow the Holy Spirit to take place in their life. These are the tribulation Saints.

In Rev 6:9-11 (NKJV) souls are seen under the altar in heaven. These are souls who have been slain for the word of God and for testifying for the word of God. These souls cried out and expressed a desire for their blood to be avenged against those who had slain them for the word of God. They were given white robes and told to arrest and await their fellow servants who would also be killed and this part would be complete. These things will all happen after the fifth seal is opened.

Rev 7:13-14 (NKJV)

The question was asked who are these arrayed in white robes and where they come from and John said to them you know these are the ones who come out of the great tribulation and washed their robes and made them white in the blood of the Lamb. It is pretty evident that these spoken of are the tribulation Saints, the hard Saints the wheat that must be crushed to line up with the word of God.

Truly the blood of Jesus will never lose its power, for even those who did not go in the rapture and yet are experiencing the tribulation have washed their robes and made them white in the blood of the Lamb. Jesus to his ultimate mercy has given them a way to stand before him.

THE GRAPES OF WRATH THESE REJECT CHRIST

The world would not receive Christ, they had no desire to be a part of him or even to be Christian. They don't believe in God and may even serve Satan or other idols in various ways. These I call the grapes of wrath. They are to be pressed. When a grape is pressed it is totally consumed and destroyed; all that is left is the essence. These who reject Christ will have to go through the winepress.

In reference to Rev 14:17-20 (NKJV) an Angel comes out of the temple which is in heaven having a sharp sickle, and this is saying that he is a reaper coming out to reap. Another angel comes from the altar with power over fire and he cries out to the one who has to sickle and tells him to thrust his sickle and gather the clusters of the vine of the earth for the grapes are fully ripe. This is speaking of the grapes of wrath. The iniquity in the air has reached its fullness and the grapes of wrath are fully ripe and ready to be reaped. The grapes of wrath are those who have totally rejected Christ. Those who are in iniquity and have no hope except to be burned in the fire. The angel who had power over the fire told the angel with the sickle to go ahead and read those of the earth who are going to burn. Those who rejected Christ.

After the Angel thrust his sickle into the earth, he gathered the vine of the earth and threw it into the great winepress of the wrath of God to be crushed. God has a winepress for those who rejected Christ. It says here that the winepress was trampled outside the city and the blood of the winepress came up to the horses bridles and for 1600 furlongs which is 1/8 of a mile.

THE FEAST OF ATONEMENT

THE FEAST OF TABERNACLES

THE UNRIGHTEOUS SHALL NOT INHERIT
THOSE WHO PRACTICE THESE THINGS SHALL NOT INHERIT GODS KINGDOM.

1 Cor 6:9-10 (KJV) Know ye not that the unrighteous shall not inherit the kingdom of God? Be not deceived: neither fornicators, nor idolaters, nor adulterers, nor effeminate, nor abusers of themselves with mankind, **10** Nor thieves, nor covetous, nor drunkards, nor revilers, nor extortioners, shall inherit the kingdom of God.
The unrighteous will not inherit the kingdom of God, but the righteous shall.

PRACTICE WHAT THINGS?

THOSE WHO PRACTICE THESE THINGS
Please make a note that the unrighteous will not inherit the kingdom of God. And let me show you those who will not receive the kingdom of God.

1 Cor 6:9-11 (KJV).
They are fornicators, idoladers, adulterers, effeminate or homosexuals, abusers with themselves with mankind, thieves, covetous, drunkards, revilers, extortioners.

YOU PRACTICED UNRIGHTEOUS THINGS

And such were some of you: but ye are washed, but ye are sanctified, but ye are justified in the name of the Lord Jesus, and by the Spirit of our God.

YOU WERE CHANGED

God the father through Jesus Christ changed you, washed you, sanctified you, justified you in the name of our Lord Jesus, and by the spirit of our God.

WHAT DO YOU PRACTICE?

RIGHTEOUS - Means to be in right standing / The ability to stand in Gods presence without guilt or shame.

TWO PARTS TO RIGHTEOUSNESS

1. **BEING MADE RIGHTEOUSNESS**
2. **WALKING IN RIGHTEOUSNESS**
3. **RIGHTEOUS dedicated, or consecrated to the service of God. Holy.**

1. PROVISIONAL RIGHTEOUSNESS

2 Cor 5:20-21 (KJV) For he hath made him *to be* sin for us, who knew no sin; **that we might be made the righteousness of God in him.**

2. RIGHTEOSNESS – A PATH (To walk in))

Prov 2:19-20 (KJV) That thou mayest walk in the way of good *men*, **and keep the paths of the righteous.**

3. WHO IS RIGHTEOUS?

Psalms 15:1-2 (KJV) He that walketh uprightly, and worketh righteousness, and speaketh the truth in his heart **dedicated, or consecrated to the service of God**

WHO HAS GONE TO HEAVEN BEFORE THE RAPTURE?

If you believe the word of God you believe in the rapture. For God has given every man a measure of faith, and his word. If it's in God's will, it's in God's word. It is not in God's will, it's not in God's word.

QUESTION :WHO HAS GONE TO HEAVEN BEFORE?
Gone to heaven without dying before the rapture

Even though others have gone to heaven before Jesus's death burial and resurrection we must understand that the past Saints who went to heaven did so on credit with Jesus. Look at Jesus as the master card and they made a purchase based on the equity behind the card. The Old Testament saints look forward to what Jesus's death burial and resurrection provided. We in the New Testament look back to what Jesus death burial and resurrection provided in history is based on his story. B. C. is before Christ and A.D. is after his death.

So no one could truly go to heaven without Jesus's resurrection from the dead. He conquered death so you don't have to. He conquered death, because no one else could.

1ST ANSWER: ENOCH

The word of God says in Genesis 5:21 – 24 that Enoch lived 65 years and begat Methuselah and Methuselah 300 years and begat sons and daughters and all the days of Enoch were 365 years. And then the word of God states that Enoch walked with God and then God took him. This is giving an emphasis on Methuselah's birth. The word Methuselah actually means it shall be seen, and I believe that it's referring to the time of the flood, when Noah built the ark. No one had seen rain up until this time. The water had come up from the ground as a missed, but the Methuselah's name means it shall be seen. The word of God says that Enoch walked with God. When the word of God in Romans eight says to walk in the spirit and you shall not fulfill the lust of the flesh, I believe to walk with God is most assuredly walking in the spirit.

Heb 11:5-6 (KJV)
But without faith *it is* impossible to please *him*: for he that cometh to God must believe that he is, and *that* he is a rewarder of them that diligently seek him.

Heb 11:5-6 (KJV) says that Enoch was translated that he should not see death. Enoch walked with God. Don't you think that if we walk with God we will not see the tribulation. The word of God says that God knows how to deliver his Saints from destruction. Don't you know that the tribulation is going to be much destruction. Enoch was no longer found in the earth because God had translated him. The word of God says that he pleased God. That is his testimony.

without faith it is impossible to please him:
for he that cometh to God must believe that he is, and that he is a
rewarder of them that diligently seek him.

IF YOU DON'T LOVE GOD
IF YOU DO NOT BELIEVE THE WORD OF GOD
IF YOU DON'T OBEY GOD
IF YOU DON'T EXERCISE IMPARTED FAITH FROM GOD.
IF YOU DON'T PLEASE GOD,
DON'T WORRY ABOUT THE RAPTURE,
BECAUSE YOU AREN'T GOING.
GOD IS PLEASED WHEN YOU **OBEY HIS WORD**

Gen 5:24 (KJV)
And Enoch walked with God: and he *was* not; for God took him.
LESSON = ENOCH PLEASED GOD

2nd ANSWER: **ELIJAH**
ELIJAH FULFILLED HIS MISSION

WHO WAS ELIJAH?

James 5:17 (KJV)
Elijah was just like any other man and he prayed that it might not rain and it didn't rain. The difference between him and most was his faith and his faithfulness. He turned his passions to God. Turning your passions to God is what makes you a man of God.

<u>Elijah trusted God. Elijah was only human like us.</u>

I realize we do not always come against 450 prophets of baal and tens of thousands of Israelites, **but we must learn to trust God.** Elijah mocked the devil when he built a fresh altar, dug a trench, put wood on it, and placed a bullock on the wood. He then had 12 Barrels of water poured on the sacrifice until the trench around the altar was filled with water.

ELIJAH TRUSTED GOD

When the time came to offer the sacrifice Elijah stepped back and prayed a short prayer. Then fire from heaven came and consumed the sacrifice, the wood, the stones, and licked up the water from the ditch. This caused God to be glorified. When the Israelites witnessed this, they remembered their God and fell on their faces and repented, and the prophets of baal were killed.

ELIJAH FINISHED HIS MISSION

Elijah taking leave of Elisha, divides Jordan with his mantle
2 Kings 2:1-12 (KJV)
And Elijah took his mantle, and wrapped *it* together, and smote the waters, and they were divided hither and thither, so that they two went over on dry ground.

ELISHA

2 Kings 2:14 (KJV) And he took the mantle of Elijah that fell from him, and smote the waters, and said, Where *is* the LORD God of Elijah?

Granting Elisha his request, Elijah is taken up by a fiery chariot.

2 Kings 2:1-11 (KJV)
Elijah and Elisha were walking and talking and all of a sudden a chariot of fire and horses of fire appeared and apparently they appeared between the two and Elijah went up to heaven in the chariot, but not before you Elijah had dropped the promised mantle to his friend and proselyte.

JESUS GRANTED THE CHURCHES REQUEST AS HE WAS TAKEN UP

Eph 4:7-8 (KJV)
Wherefore he saith, When he ascended up on high, he led captivity captive, and gave gifts unto men

WHEN JESUS WAS TAKEN UP

Even though Jesus being taken up to heaven after Enoch and Elijah, there would have been no translation to heaven of Enoch and Elijah without Jesus' death burial and resurrection from the dead, even though they were translated before Jesus came into the earth.

Notice: Elijah went up to heaven and gave a great gift to Elisha. We as the church also received a great gift but it was when Jesus the one who made it possible for even Elijah to go to heaven without dying, rose and went to heaven, giving gifts to men, and leaving captivity captive.

Jesus will return the same way

Acts 1:9-11 (KJV)

And when he had spoken these things, while they beheld, he was taken up; and a cloud received him out of their sight. And while they looked stedfastly toward heaven as he went up, behold, two men stood by them in white apparel; Which also said, Ye men of Galilee, why stand ye gazing up into heaven? this same Jesus, which is taken up from you into heaven, shall so come in like manner as ye have seen him go into heaven.

Thank God for Enoch's attributes. He walked with God.
Thank God for Elijah's attributes. He trusted God.
Thank God for Jesus. He walked with God, trusted God, and **saved the world because he is God. HALLELUAH!**

1 Cor 15:47-50 (KJV)
The first man is of the earth, earthy: the second man is the Lord from heaven. As is the earthy, such are they also that are earthy: and as is the heavenly, such are they also that are heavenly. And as we have borne the image of the earthy, we shall also bear the image of the heavenly. Now this I say, brethren, that flesh and blood cannot inherit the kingdom of God; neither doth corruption inherit incorruption.

1 Cor 15:47-50 (KJV) this passage of Scripture is saying that the first man is of the earth speaking of Adam. Adam was formed of the dust of the earth and he was made a living soul. This same verse is saying that Jesus is the second man and as the Lord from heaven. And from the earthy man came the whole earth of earthy men and women, but from the second man who was heavenly we who are of the earth had to be born again into this heavenly man. Because we were formed of the dust of the earth, we are from this planet, but because we received Jesus Christ as Savior we have now also become a part of him and are recipients of where he came from; heaven. We have borne the image of the people of Earth, and the earthy. We shall also bear the

image of the heavenly, for we shall be changed 1 COR 15:51 – 54 Behold, I shew you a mystery; We shall not all sleep, but we shall all be changed, In a moment, in the twinkling of an eye, at the last trump: for the trumpet shall sound, and the dead shall be raised incorruptible, and we shall be changed. For this corruptible must put on incorruption, and this mortal must put on immortality. So when this corruptible shall have put on incorruption, and this mortal shall have put on immortality.

As you see when *we are changed immortality will become ours and when we change incorruption will become ours. In other words we will have a glorified body.*

We shall also bear the image of the heavenly

Flesh and blood cannot inherit the kingdom of God. Even though we are earthly, and even though the first man Adam was earthly, there is left no way for us to become heavenly except through Jesus Christ who came from heaven. Although we are earthy, through him we also become heavenly and therefore we are not just redeemed in the earth, but we are redeemed to heaven.

NEXT IS THE GREAT MULTITUDE

The Tribulation Saints.
Rev 7:8-17 (KJV)

After this I beheld, and, lo, a great multitude, which no man could number, of all nations, and kindreds, and people, and tongues, stood before the throne, and before the Lamb, clothed with white robes, and palms in their hands;

10 And cried with a loud voice, saying, Salvation to our God which sitteth upon the throne, and unto the Lamb. **11** And all the angels stood round about the throne, and *about* the elders and the four beasts, and fell before the throne on their faces, and worshipped God, **12** Saying,

Amen: Blessing, and glory, and wisdom, and thanksgiving, and honour, and power, and might, *be* unto our God for ever and ever. Amen. **13** And one of the elders answered, saying unto me, **What are these which are arrayed in white robes? and whence came they? 14** And I said unto him, Sir, thou knowest. And he said to me, **These are they which came out of great tribulation, and have washed their robes, and made them white in the blood of the Lamb. 15** Therefore are they before the throne of God, and serve him day and night in his temple: and he that sitteth on the throne shall dwell among them. **16** They shall hunger no more, neither thirst any more; neither shall the sun light on them, nor any heat. **17** For the Lamb which is in the midst of the throne shall feed them, and shall lead them unto living fountains of waters: and God shall wipe away all tears from their eyes.

These Saints are the wheat that was spoken of who for some reason did not sit under the teaching and admonition of the Lord, but now their devotion and faith has skyrocketed because of their zeal and of being committed to God and having given their lives for the Lamb, and washing their roles in the blood of the Lamb, they are ready as any for heaven.

THE 144,000

If you will notice the Bible deals with three groups of people.

The Jew, the Gentiles, and the church. Did you notice that at the end of the book of Revelation, chapter three, that the holy church, those who had seperated themselves from the world system, in right standing with Christ, paying attention to keep His word, and who were watching and waiting for Christ had disappeared.

And notice: the words that began the fourth chapter of revelations.

Rev 4:1 (KJV)

After this I looked, and, behold, a door *was* opened in heaven: and the first voice which I heard *was* as it were of a trumpet talking with me; which said, **Come up hither, and I will shew thee things which must be hereafter**

The one hundred and forty four thousand(144,000) are Jewish evangelists and are mentioned in the book of Revelation, Chapter 7 These are God's Elect

Rev 7:1-4 (KJV) *Notice in Revelation 4 a door was open to heaven in the voice was heard as it were a trumpet that said come up hither I'm going to show you things that must be hereafter. Now who scroll down to Revelation 71 we see that the Angels in the four corners of the earth are holding back the four winds of the earth that the wind should not blow on the earth mourn the sea or on any tree. The number four is the number of the earth. Now we see an Angel ascending from the East with the seal of God and he cries a loud voice to the four Angels double was given to hurt the earth and the sea, now this Angel says not to hurt anything until the servants of God has God seal of God on there foreheads.*

And how many of these servants were there: 144,000.

GOD SAID; NOT UNTIL MINE ARE SAFE

The Angels were saying, Hurt not the earth, neither the sea, nor the trees, till we have sealed the servants of our God in their foreheads

The Lamb stands on Mount Zion with the company of His elect

Rev 14:1-5

a Lamb stood on mount Zion with the 144,000 servants having the father's name written on therefore heads. There was a voice from heaven as the voice of many waters and the voice of great thunder and harpers were harping and they sung a new song before the throne and before the beast and the elders no one could learn the song but the hut the 144,000 which were redeemed from the earth. These 144,000 servants have never been defiled with women. They are virgins. They follow the Lamb wherever he goes. They were taken out a from among men, being the firstfruits unto God and to the Lamb. In their mouth is no guile because they are without fault before God.

THE TWO WITNESSES

WHO ARE THE TWO WITNESSES?
LETS LOOK CLOSLY AT WHAT THEY DO.

These two witnesses are actually returning after there first translation from earth to heaven to fulfill Gods last day mission.

Abraham had said to the rich man in hell that even if Moses returned from the dead the people would not listen. **HERE IS PROOF.**

Luke 16:31 (KJV) And Abraham said; unto him, If they hear not Moses and the prophets, neither will they be persuaded, though one rose from the dead.

God is so merciful that he continually send witnesses. He does not wish that any should perish. He sends to the earth his word over and over and over again.

The Two Witnesses

Rev 11:3-12 (KJV)
And I will give *power* unto my two witnesses, and they shall prophesy a thousand two hundred *and* threescore days, clothed in sackcloth. **These are the two olive trees, and the two candlesticks standing before the God of the earth.**

OLIVE TREE= ANOINTED
CANDLE STICKS = HOLY

And if any man will hurt them, fire proceedeth out of their mouth, and devoureth their enemies: and if any man will hurt them, he must in this manner be killed.

TO COME AGAINST THEM IS TO DIE

These have power to shut heaven, that it rain not in the days of their prophecy:

THEY CAN CAUSE IT NOT TO RAIN

and have power over waters to turn them to blood, and to smite the earth with all plagues, as often as they will.

THEY CAN TURN WATER INTO BLOOD AND SMITE THE EARTH WITH ALL PLAGUES

THE BEAST FROM THE BOTTOMLESS PIT WILL KILL THEM. THEY WILL LAY IN THE STREET THREE AND A HALF DAYS, IN THE PLACE **WHERE OUR LORD WAS CRUCIFIED.**

And their dead bodies *shall lie* **in the street of the great city,**
which spiritually is called Sodom and Egypt, where also our Lord was crucified. And they of the people and kindreds and tongues and nations shall see their dead bodies three days and an half, and shall not suffer their dead bodies to be put in graves.

WHERE OUR LORD WAS CRUCIFIED.

THEY SHALL NOT EVEN BURY THEM

And they that dwell upon the earth shall rejoice over them, and make merry, and shall send gifts one to another; because these two prophets tormented them that dwelt on the earth.

THOSE OF THE EARTH SHALL REJOICE OVER THEIR DEATH.
THEY SHALL MAKE MERRY AND GIVE EACH OTHER GIFTS.

THEY ARE GLAD THEY DON'T HAVE TO HEAR THE WORD OF GOD.

Come up hither

After three days these two men will be raised up from the street and they will stand on your feet and great fear will come upon those who see them and they will hear a great voice from heaven saying come up hither and these men will be taken up into heaven.

WHEN THE LIFE FROM GOD ENTERED THEM GREAT FEAR CAME UPON THE PEOPLE.
THE ENEMY SEE THEM.

TYPES OF DELIVERANCE FROM TRIBULATIONS AND EARTHS DESTRUCTION
ONLY THE OBEDIENT TO GOD SHALL LIVE

AS IT WAS IN THE DAYS OF NOAH

Matt 24:37-39
But as the days of Noe *were*, so shall also the coming of the Son of man be. **38** For as in the days that were before the flood they were eating and drinking, marrying and giving in marriage, until the day that Noe entered into the ark, **39** And knew not until the flood came, and took them all away; so shall also the coming of the Son of man be.

AS IT WAS IN THE DAYS OF LOT

Luke 17:27-33
Likewise also as it was in the days of Lot; they did eat, they drank, they bought, they sold, they planted, they builded; **29** But the same day that Lot went out of Sodom it rained fire and brimstone from heaven, and destroyed *them* all. **30** Even thus shall it be in the day

when the Son of man is revealed. **31** In that day, he which shall be upon the housetop, and his stuff in the house, let him not come down to take it away: and he that is in the field, let him likewise not return back. **32** **Remember Lot's wife.** **33** Whosoever shall seek to save his life shall lose it; and whosoever shall lose his life shall preserve it.

THIS IS SAID OF NOAHS DAY

But as the days of Noe were, so shall also the coming of the Son of man be. For as in the days that were before the flood they were eating and drinking, marrying and giving in marriage, until the day that Noe entered into the ark, And knew not until the flood came, and took them all away; so shall also the coming of the Son of man be.

THIS WILL BE SAID OF THE CHURCH

During the coming of the Son of Man the people were eating and drinking, marrying and giving in marriage, until the day that the church was caught up in the air with Christ, and the tribulation caught them unaware and **those left behind knew not until the tribulation came.**

**MAKE YOUR INVESTMENTS IN HEAVEN
GET CLOTHED OR DRESSED
MAKE SURE YOU CAN SEE**

GOOD COUNSEL

Rev 3:18 (KJV)
18 I counsel thee to buy of me gold tried in the fire, that thou mayest be rich**; and white raiment, that thou mayest be clothed,** and *that* the shame of thy nakedness do not appear; and anoint thine eyes with eyesalve, that thou mayest see.

WILL YOU BE
DRESSED FOR THE WEDDING?
AND THEY WILL ENTER THE KINGDOM OF GOD
Isaiah 61:10 (NKJV) I will greatly rejoice in the Lord,
My soul shall be joyful in my God;
For He has clothed me with **the garments of salvation,**
He has covered me with **the robe of righteousness,**

MY GARMENT

2 Cor 5:21 (KJV) For he hath made him *to be* sin for us, who knew no sin; that we might be made the righteousness of God in him.

YOU MUST KEEP YOUR GARMENT

Rev 16:15 (KJV)
Behold, I come as a thief. Blessed *is* he that watcheth, **and keepeth his garments, lest he walk naked, and they see his shame.**

MY ROBE

Psalms 25:4 (KJV) Shew me thy ways, O LORD; teach me thy paths.

THESE WILL NOT GO TO HEAVEN

THESE ARE CONTRARY TO THE SPIRIT OF GOD
1 Cor 6:9-10 (KJV)
Know ye not that the unrighteous shall not inherit the kingdom of God? Be not deceived: neither fornicators, nor idolaters, nor adulterers, nor effeminate, nor abusers of themselves with mankind, **10** Nor thieves, nor covetous, nor drunkards, nor revilers, nor extortioners, shall inherit the kingdom of God.

FORNICATION - Sexual intercourse between people who are not married to each other.

IDOLATRY - Serving or worshipping Idols (literally or figuratively)

ADULTERY = voluntary sexual relations between a married person with a person who is not his or her spouse.

EFFIMINATE - A person who allows himself to be sexually abused contrary to nature. Fetishes of self abuse etc. A homosexual or sodomite. One who collaborates with, or desires one of the same sex.

ABUSERS OF THEMSELVES WITH MANKIND - A man who lies in bed with another man. A homosexual. **(A male)**

THIEVES - One who steals. Those who take what is not theirs.

COVETOUS -To desire wrongfully, inordinately, or without due regard for the rights of other

DRUNKARD - One given to intoxication. Under the influence. An intoxication can be even with the influence of Sin. (The world)

REVILERS - railers, persecuters, blasphemers, or insulters.

EXTORTIONERS - One who steals or robs publicly. A rapacious person. A violent one; aggressive as a thief, or one who steals secretly or deliberately.

18 But if you are led by the Spirit, you are not under the law.

WALK IN THE SPIRIT

and you will keep the 10 Commandments

Gal 5:16-23 (NKJV) I say then: Walk in the Spirit, and you shall not fulfill the lust of the flesh. 17 For the flesh lusts against the Spirit, and the Spirit against the flesh; and these are contrary to one another, so that you do not do the things that you wish. 18 But if you are led by the Spirit, you are not under the law.

WORKS OF THE FLESH

19 Now the works of the flesh are evident, which are: adultery, fornication, uncleanness, lewdness, 20 idolatry, sorcery, hatred, contentions, jealousies, outbursts of wrath, selfish ambitions, dissensions, heresies, 21 envy, murders, drunkenness, revelries, and the like; of which I tell you beforehand, just as I also told you in time past, that <u>those who practice such things will not inherit the kingdom of God.</u>

Repent and be washed

Gal 5:19-21

<u>17 MENTIONED WORKS OF THE FLESH</u>

ADULTERY = voluntary sexual relations between a married person to a person who is not his or her spouse.

FORNICATION = sexual intercourse between people who are not married to each other.

UNCLEANESS = morally impure, evil; vile. The opposite of holy.

LASCIVIOUSNESS = an indication of sexual interest or expression of lust or lewdness; a lascivious gesture.

IDOLATRY = worship of idols, fetishism, reverence or adoration to something or someone other than God.

WITCHCRAFT = rebellion unto God by exercising spell craft, magic, skills and abilities that override someone else's will and even by esoteric secret knowledge, normally accompanied by demons.

HATRED = intense dislike or ill will.

VARIANCE = the factor quality of being different, divergent, or inconsistent.

EMULATIONS = a rivalry created by ambition or in the to endeavor to equal or Excel above another, even your teacher.

WRATH = a strong start were fierce anger; deeply resentful indignation.

STRIFE = a bitter sometimes violent conflict or dissension. A very angrier violent disagreement between two or more people or a group.

SEDITIONS = conduct or speech inciting people to rebel against the authority of a state, monarch, or institution

HERESIES = heresies any provocative belief with theory that is strongly in variance with the established belief or customs. A heretic is one who makes such claims or beliefs.

ENVYINGS = a feeling of discontent or covetousness with regard to another's advantages, success, possessions, or even his person.

MURDERS = the crime of unlawfully killing a person especially with malice of forethought. It even begins with a thought, and in the thought process.

DRUNKENESS = the state of being intoxicated. Under the influence. An intoxication can be even with the influence of Sin. (The world)

REVELLINGS = to take great pleasure or delight, carousing, orgies, and usually in worldly excess and/or luxury. Also enjoying tumult, confusion, and large masses of people. Worldly celebration.

Gal 5:19-21

Now the works of the flesh are manifest, which are *these*; Adultery, fornication, uncleanness, lasciviousness, **20** Idolatry, witchcraft, hatred, variance, emulations, wrath, strife, seditions, heresies, **21** Envyings, murders, drunkenness, revellings, and such like: of the which I tell you before, as I have also told *you* in time past, that they which do such things shall not inherit the kingdom of God.

BUT YOU ARE

WASHED, SANCTIFIED, AND JUSTIFIED

WASHED = to be made clean, by the washing and regeneration of the word. The word regenerates when it washes.(Sin degenerates)

SANCTIFIED = set aside and declared as holy

JUSTIFIED = to be made right before God

YOU WERE WASHED

For those of you who think they are going to hell or may miss the rapture because of these things that have been in your life, the next Scripture says:

1 Cor 6:11 (KJV) This passage of Scripture is saying that every one who has become a child of God has been washed, and sanctified, and justified in the name of the Lord Jesus, and by God. You are no longer a part of the group that will not enter the kingdom of God.

DO = PRACTICE

DO: this word do in the original language, is saying; they which practice such things as mentioned in **1 Cor 6:9** shall not inherit the kingdom of God. You were washed, when you repented, and to repent means to be sorry and to go the other way. If you don't go the other way then you continue to practice.

AND, IF YOU SLIP

GO TO **1 John 1:9**
1 John 1:8-10 (KJV)
If we continue to sin, and even if we practice sin unvoluntarily to say we have no sin is a lie and we are accusing God. The best thing for us to do was confess our sins, knowingly and unknowingly. Once we confess sin God is faithful and just to forgive us our sins, and to cleanse us from all unrighteousness.

KEEP YOUR GARMENT CLEAN, OR REPENT

Rev 16:15 (KJV
Truly watching for the return of Christ and keeping your garment is the most important thing you can do other than prayer. The word of God says that if you do not watch for Jesus's return, and if you do not keep your garment you will surely walk in nakedness and shame.

WASHED

Titus 3:3-7 (this Scripture tells how foolish we were. It tells how disobedient, deceived self-serving and lustful we were we were living with malice and envy hate, and hating one another. It says but the love of God our Savior toward man appeared not by works of righteousness which we've done but according to his mercy he saved us. We were renewed by the Holy Ghost and the washing and regeneration which he shed on us abundantly through

Jesus Christ our Savior. We were also justified by his grace that we should be heirs according to the hope of eternal life.

WASHING OF WATER BY THE WORD

Eph 5:25-27

This Scripture shows that Christ loves us. He conveys it in a way that we can relate to. He says as a husband loves his wife even also Christ loves the church. Through his love peace sanctify and cleanse is set with the washing of water by the word. Jesus his soul purpose is to present to himself a glorious church not having wrinkle, spot, or any such thing, and that it should be holy and without blame.

ACCESS BY FAITH INTO GRACE

Romans 5:1-5 (KJV) <u>Therefore being justified by faith, we have peace with God through our Lord Jesus Christ:</u> 2 By whom also we have access by faith into this grace wherein we stand**<u>, and rejoice in hope of the glory of God.</u>** 3 And not only so, but we glory in tribulations also: knowing that tribulation worketh patience; 4 And patience, experience; and experience, hope: 5 And hope maketh not ashamed; because the love of God is shed abroad in our hearts by the Holy Ghost which is given unto us.

PEACE

Therefore being justified by faith, we have peace with God through our Lord Jesus Christ:

HE WHO HAS THE FRUIT OF THE SPIRIT?

Gal 5:22 But the fruit of the spirit is love, joy, peace, long-suffering, kindness, goodness, faithfulness, gentleness, self-control,

If these characteristics are in your character no law can come against you to stop you from inheriting the kingdom of God.

WHO HAS PREPARED TO BE THE BRIDE?
A BRIDE MUST PREPARE
JESUS HAS AN ESPOUSED BRIDE SHE IS TO BE A VIRGIN

Matt 25:1-13
It had always been Jewish custom that the espoused bride be a virgin. It's only logical that Jesus his bride also be a virgin. Jesus is bride is to come in the church and to be born again. We as the church are justified and justification means that we are just as if we had never sinned. A person who is never sinned has the heart of a virgin. In God's eyes whether we are foolish virgins or wise virgins, we are all from the family of God because of salvation, and we are virgins. Whether we sleep or are awake we are virgins. Virgins await the cry of the bridegroom. When they hear; the bridegroom cometh it is time to pick up their lamps that also have oil, trimmed their lamps, and go for to meet the bridegroom. Even though the foolish virgins had no oil they were still virgins, but the wise virgins became the bride. This shows that many of the virgins, many of the saved, many of the born again Christians will not be a part of the bride because they are foolish. The bride is reserved for those who have prepare as they await for the bridegroom.

BUT SHE MUST HAVE A LAMP WITH OIL

Take a look at these VIRGINS
Matt 25:1 The 10 virgins all had lamps, and all went out to meet the bridegroom.

five were wise

Matt 25:4 The difference between the wise and the foolish was that the wise took oil in their lamps.

five were foolish

Matt 25:2-3) Those who were foolish took their lamps and took no oil with them

they all slumbered and slept
Matt 25:4-5 But while the bridegroom was delayed, they all slumbered and slept

they all trimmed their lamps / TO TRIM IS TO PREPARE. They all trimmed their lamps – this mean to adorn oneself.

Matt 25:6-7 go out to meet him!' Then all those virgins arose and trimmed their lamps. The wise are those who were prepared ready and apparently had been watching for his return.

TRIM = ADORN / to arrange one's self in proper order

the foolish asked the wise for oil / THEY HAD TIME TO PREPARE, BUT WASTED IT. It looks as if the foolish virgins were not attentive to hope. If they expected him why did they not go out and get oil early. They just went with the flow and slept even though their lamps were not full.

Matt 25:8 (NKJV) And the foolish said to the wise, 'Give us some of your oil, for our lamps are going out. **Don't prepare for your eternity the way these foolish virgins did.**

The wise said "no" / THIS IS FOR ETERNITY, AND TO BE MARRIED TO THE LAMB OF GOD.

Matt 25:8-9 But the wise answered, saying, 'No, lest there should not be enough for us and you; but go rather to those who sell, and buy for yourselves

WHAT WOULD YOU HAVE SAID?

The foolish went to buy oil
Matt 25:9-10 (NKJV) And while they went to buy, the bridegroom came, and those who were ready went in with him to the wedding; and the door was shut.

The bridegroom came
Matt 25:9-10 (NKJV) And while they went to buy, the bridegroom came, and those who were ready went in with him to the wedding; and **the door was shut.**

Those who were ready went with him
The foolish came and said Lord open up let us In
ARE YOU READY?

FIVE FOOLISH

WE HAVE PEOPLE IN THE CHURCH WHO ARE WAITING FOR THE RAPTURE AND ARE NOT PREPARING, NOR HAVE PLANS OF BEING PREPARED. THEY THINK THE RAPTURE IS FOR THE WHOLE FAMILY OF GOD, PREPARED OR UNPREPARED. **YOU HAVE TO BE DRESSED FOR THE WEDDING.**

GET FILLED NOW

BE READY, BE PREPARED, GET YOUR OIL NOW, AND IF YOU SLUMBER YOU'LL WAKE WITH OIL FILL YOUR LAMP NOW, IS YOUR WICK TRIMMED?

Psalms 119:105 (KJV)
Thy word *is* a lamp unto my feet, and a light unto my path.

Matt 25:6-7 (KJV)
Then all those virgins arose, and trimmed their lamps.
Trim wick = to adorn ones self

ARE YOU DRESSED?

Matt 22:1-14
This is a parable and in so many words this parable is describing what the kingdom of heaven will be like when we get there. This particular parable says that a certain King set up a marriage for his son, and when the King came to see the guests he saw that there was a man who was not dressed or prepared for the wedding. He said to the man why did you come not having a wedding garment, and the man was speechless. The King said to the servants bind him hand and foot and take him away, and cast him into outer darkness with there will be weeping and gnashing of teeth. For many are called but few are chosen.

We must understand that JESUS PAID FOR A ROBE OF RIGHTEOUSNES, SENT THE HOLY SPIRIT TO HELP YOU GET DRESSED. BUT THERE WILL ALWAYS BE SOME THAT WON'T EVEN PUT IT ON.

THE NEW NORMAL IS:
SMOKING, FIGHTING, CURSING, COMMITTING ADULTERY, PARTYING, FORNICATION, SHACKING, WHOREMONGERING, (HOMOSEXUAL, AND LESBIANS) AND EXPECTING TO GO TO HEAVEN

WHO IS DRESSED WITH THE PURCHASED WEDDING GARMENT?

IT IS PAID FOR BY THE PRECIOUS BLOOD OF JESUS?

No wedding garment; no wedding.

GET DRESSED
JESUS PURCHASED THE WEDDING GARMENT
I KNOW YOU ARE SAVED, BUT YOU WON'T DISHONOR
GOD BY GOING TO HIS SONS WEDDING; NOT PROPERLY
DRESSED.

Adorn yourself inwardly

ADORN= to command oneself
YOU WOULD NOT GO TO THE GREATEST EVENT IN
HISTORY IN YOUR GYM CLOTHES WOULD YOU?

Job 29:14 (KJV)
I put on righteousness, and it clothed me: my judgment *was* as a robe and a diadem.

Righteousness is my clothing, and my judgment is the adorning which is my robe and diadem.

Rev 19:8 (KJV)
And to her was granted that she should be arrayed in fine linen, clean and white: for the fine linen is the righteousness of saints.

You must be granted to be arrayed in fine linen because this is the theme of the wedding: the righteousness of the Saints

DENY UNGODLY LUST

Titus 2:11-14

says that the grace of God that brings salvation has appeared to all men. Grace is God giving you what you don't deserve. Grace taught us that denying ungodliness and worldly lusts we should live soberly, righteously, and godly in this present age. We are to continue look for the blessed hope and glorious appearing of God and our Savior Jesus Christ. He gave himself for us to purify us redeem us from lawless deeds, make assists special people, zealous of good works.

DO THE WILL OF THE FATHER

Matthew 7: 21

It's easy to say Lord Lord and expecting her into the kingdom of heaven, but God says it's only those who do the will of my father who will enter heaven. Many will say did not prophesied in your name, cast out devils in your name, and done many wonders in your name? The Lord will declare to them, I never knew you; depart from me you wicked doers.

QUESTION : WHAT IS THE WILL OF THE FATHER? ANSWER: TO WALK IN RIGHTEOUSNESS.

Rev 16:15 (KJV)
Behold, I come as a thief. Blessed *is* he that watcheth, and keepeth his garments, lest he walk naked, and they see his shame.

BE WISE. BUILD YOUR HOUSE ON THE ROCK JESUS IS THE ROCK

Matt 7:21-27
Build your house on the rock in that way when the rain comes in the flood, and the wind blows and beat on that house; it will not fall because is founded on the rock critic and build your house on the sand and the rain comes in the flood comes, and the wind blows and beats on the house and the house falls, it will be a great fall.

OBEY GOD NOW. DON'T WAIT FOR THE RAIN TO DESCEND, OR THE FLOODS TO COME, OR THE WIND TO BLOW.

*ABOVE ALL; **BUILD YOUR HOUSE ON THE ROCK. (THE WORD OF GOD)***

BE COUNTED WORTHY

Luke 21:36
We must watch and pray the purpose of being counted worthy to escape the tribulation, and to be able to stand before the Son of Man.

WE MUST WALK ACCORDING TO THE SPIRIT

Romans 8:1-2
If we walk in the spirit we will not fulfill the lust of the flesh, and to walk in the spirit is to walk in righteousness, and as we walk in righteousness we are in right standing with God. We have the ability to stand in gods presence without guilt and without shame. So walk in the spirit.

WE MUST MAKE OUR ELECTION SURE

TO WALK ACCORDING TO THE SPIRIT IS TO WALK IN THE WORD - and because the anointing is on the word, the oil for your lamp is produced.

To walk in the false word, and or the works of the flesh you produce only sin and death.

QUESTION: WHO WILL GO IN THE RAPTURE?
ANSWER: THOSE WHO ARE READY.

QUESTION: WHO WILL BE THE BRIDE?
ANSWER: THOSE WHO HAVE MADE THEMSELVES READY.

ADORN = ANOTHER DEFINITION / to trim the wick

THE BRIDE HAS MADE HERSELF READY

Have you ever seen a bride on this occasion, not prepared
Rev 19:7 (KJV)
Let us be glad and rejoice, and give honour to him: for the marriage of the Lamb is come, and his wife hath made herself ready

"Rev 19:6-8
*A bride on this occasion will make every effort to be prepared. This is her wedding. Why do most of the church think that they can be nonchalant and attend the wedding? As a part of the bride you must make yourself ready and then you will be granted to be arrayed in fine linen clean and bright, for the fine linen is the righteous acts of the Saints. If you don't have any righteous acts you will not be granted to be arrayed in fine linen, because you will not be ready. The name of this book is, **Rapture Ready**. The rapture is for the bride.*

Why does most of the church think that the whole church is going in the Rapture?

This man didn't bother to get dressed

Matt 22:1-14 (KJV)
And Jesus answered and spake unto them again by parables, and said, The kingdom of heaven is like unto a certain king, which made a marriage for his son, And sent forth his servants to call them that were bidden to the wedding: and they would not come.

Jesus parable is of a certain King who made a marriage for son but when he came to see the guests, there was a man who did not have a wedding garment on: and he said to him, friend why did you come to the wedding without a wedding garment. And he was speechless. *I believe when the father come to see the guests there are going to be a lot of speechless Christians, because they did not prepare they did not keep their garments, or they did not get dressed for the wedding.*

And when the king came in to see the guests, he saw there a man which had not on a wedding garment: And he saith unto him, Friend, how camest thou in hither not having a wedding garment? And he was speechless. Then said the king to the servants, Bind him hand and foot, and take him away, and cast *him* into outer darkness; there shall be weeping and gnashing of teeth. For many are called, but few *are* chosen.

Chosen out of those who were called.

Preparation

REMEMBER THE OIL THE WISE VIRGIN HAD? BAPTISED MEANS TO BE FILLED TO OVERFLOW IN THE HOLY SPIRIT

Acts 1:4-5 (NKJV) And being assembled together with them, He commanded them not to depart from Jerusalem, but to wait for the Promise of the Father, "which," He said, "you have heard from Me; 5 for John truly baptized with water, but **you shall be baptized with the Holy Spirit not many days from now."**

THEY WERE ALL FILLED (BAPTIZED)

An act of God

Acts 2:1-4 (NKJV) When the Day of Pentecost had fully come, they were all with one accord in one place. 2 And suddenly there came a sound from heaven, as of a rushing mighty wind, and it filled the whole house where they were sitting. 3 Then there appeared to them divided tongues, as of fire, and one sat upon each of them. **4 And they were all filled with the Holy Spirit and began to speak with other tongues,** as the Spirit gave them utterance.

BAPTISM = TO BE EMERGED

There is truly **one baptism** *but* **many refillings and infillings**. *This is the first time the Holy Spirit appeared in this operation of the spirit, which was to filll God's people with himself.*

Thank God, he does things in simplicity to help us to comprehend his word, and to receive the promises he has given to us.

And I'm thankful that there is more than one way to be filled with the spirit of God. Let me show you some of these ways.

HERE IS A COMMAND

be not drunk with wine but be thou filled with the spirit

Eph 5:17-21 (NKJV) *Therefore do not be unwise, but understand what the will of the Lord is.* **18 And do not be drunk with wine, in which is dissipation; but be filled with the Spirit,** *19 speaking to one another in psalms and hymns and spiritual songs, singing and making melody in your heart to the Lord, 20 giving thanks always for all things to God the Father in the name of our Lord Jesus Christ, 21 submitting to one another in the fear of God.*

but be filled with the Spirit
MEANING / continue to be filled.

THE COMMAND IS / BE FILLED WITH THE HOLY SPIRIT

BEING TRUE TO THE WORD / BE CONTINUOUSLY FILLED
(SO THAT YOU ARE NEVER EMPTY)
This scripture is saying don't let your lamp go out. Continue to constantly be filled with this oil.

DIFFERENCE BETWEEN BEING BAPTIZED AND BEING FILLED

ONCE BAPTIZED IN THE HOLY SPIRIT, YOU ARE TO BE CONTINUALLY FILLED

WHAT HAPPENS WHEN FILLED?

This is the will of God. Once filled with the Holy Spirit we will begin speaking to one another in psalms, hymns and spiritual songs making melody in our hearts to the Lord. Being filled with the Holy Spirit makes you thankful always for all things. You give praise to God the father, in the name of our Lord Jesus Christ. Because we are spirit-filled, we don't mind submitting to one another in the fear of God.

When filled with the Holy Ghost you will talk like the Holy Ghost. The Holy Ghost or Holy Spirit speaks in Psalms, hymns, and spiritual songs. The Holy Spirit makes melody in his heart to the Lord. Being filled with the Holy Spirit makes you joyful and always thankful for all things. You give praises to God the father, and in the name of our Lord Jesus Christ.

WHEN THE HOLY SPIRIT CAME UPON JESUS
HE IMMEDIATELY WENT TO A WEDDING

Jesus was baptized by the Holy Spirit and went to a wedding.

John 2:2-10 (NKJV) And when they ran out of wine, the mother of Jesus said to Him, "They have no wine." 4 Jesus said to her, "Woman, what does your concern have to do with Me? My hour has not yet come." 5 His mother said to the servants, "Whatever He says to you, do it." 6 Now there were set there six waterpots of stone, according to the manner of purification of the Jews, containing twenty or thirty gallons apiece. 7 Jesus said to them, "Fill the waterpots with water." And they filled them up to the brim. 8 And He said to them, "Draw some out now, and take it to the master of the feast." And they took it. 9 When the master of the feast had tasted the water that was made wine, and did not know where it came from (but the servants who had drawn the water knew), the master of the feast called the bridegroom. 10 **And he said to him, "Every man at the beginning sets out the good wine, and when the guests have well drunk, then the inferior. <u>You have kept the good wine until now!</u>"**

The good wine is the covenant of the bride of Christ. the covenant of The church of was given last, when normally the best wine at a wedding is given first. I believe this last day covenant that was given to the church is the greatest, because it is a contract between Jesus and his bride. The new wine was symbolic of the covenant and showed the best wine was presented last.

Jesus was baptized with the Holy Spirit and went to a wedding. This shows that Jesus is wedding conscious. This shows how long-suffering he is awaiting the wedding between himself and his bride.

Notice: JESUS SAID; MY TIME IS NOT YET
John 2:24 Jesus said to her, "Woman, what does your concern have to do with Me? My hour has not yet come."
It appears as though Jesus is saying: woman your concern is this earthly wedding, but my concern is my heavenly wedding.
Notice: JESUS HAD PREVIOUSLY SAID

Matt 26:28-29 (NKJV) But I say to you, I will not drink of this fruit of the vine from now on until that day when I drink it new with you in My Father's kingdom."

There is often been a dispute and question as to whether Jesus drink wine. Yes he drink wine, but in Matthew 26:28 – 29 he said he will not drink wine again until he drink it new with us in his father's kingdom.

HOW TO GET REFILLED

To stay filled with the Holy Spirit is the key to keeping oil in your lamp. This is how you will find your way to Jesus when the trumpet sounds.

FORSAKE NOT YOUR FELLOWSHIP

Heb 10:24-25
We are to not forsake our fellowship with other believers when we see an opportunity to fellowship and assemble ourselves together we should do so. We may not need to be edified but others do at this point. Or others may not need to be edified but you may at this point. So we should not forsake their fellowship if not for any other reason but to exchange strengths.

THEY WERE BAPTIZED/ THEY WERE FILLED

*Acts 13:51-52 (NKJV) And the disciples were filled with joy and with the Holy Spirit. This passage of Scripture says the disciples were filled with joy and with the Holy Spirit, and this shows that joy is the strength of my salvation.

THEY WERE **CONTINUALLY** FILLED

***Acts 13:52 (MontgomeryNT) As for the disciples, **they were continually filled with joy**, and with the Holy Spirit.*
The Montgomery New Testament says: that the disciples were continually filled with joy and with the Holy Spirit.

Eph 5:18
And be not drunk with wine, wherein is excess; but be filled with the Spirit;

the rightful interpretation of this is: don't be a gladness with wine, and on over drink, but continually be filled with the Holy Spirit.

BE CONTINUALLY FILLED WITH THE HOLY SPIRIT

This means that you can get filled with overflowing not just one time but you can continually be filled with the Holy Spirit. There are ways to continually be filled with the Holy Spirit. Let me show you how.

HOW TO GET REFILLED
(FILL YOUR LAMP)
I am going to show you the manner in which the Holy Spirit is received, and that you may continually be filled.

*1. Suddenly, and while sitting and expecting the Holy Spirit to come. **Acts 2:1 – 4***

TO BE BAPTIZED

THE BAPTISM OF THE HOLY SPIRIT
ONE BAPTISM; MANY FILLINGS

Acts 2:1-4 (NKJV) When the Day of Pentecost had fully come, they were all with one accord in one place. 2 And suddenly there came a sound from heaven, as of a rushing mighty wind, and it filled the whole house where they were sitting. 3 Then there appeared to them divided tongues, as of fire, and one sat upon each of them. 4 And they were all filled with the Holy Spirit and began to speak with other tongues, as the Spirit gave them utterance.

TO BE FILLED
ANOTHER WAY

2. ***Instantly and unexpectedly, while listening to a sermon.*** *Acts 10:44 – 46 while these men were specifically expecting the Holy Spirit to come in one manner, they at least had an expectant attitude and their hearts were open to whatever the Holy Spirit had to say.*

ANOTHER WAY
Acts 10:44-47 *When the word of God is spoken, and when the word of God is heard.*

ANOTHER FILLING
Acts 10:44-47 (NKJV) ***While Peter was still speaking these words, the Holy Spirit fell upon all those who heard the word.*** *45 And those of the circumcision who believed were astonished, as many as came with Peter, because the gift of the Holy Spirit had been **poured out on the Gentiles also.** 46 For they heard them speak with tongues and magnify God. Then Peter answered, 47*

ANOTHER WAY
*3. **Through prayer and laying** on of the apostles hands acts 8:14 – 17; 9:17; 19:6.*

ANOTHER FILLING
Acts 8:14-17 (NKJV) *Now when the apostles who were at Jerusalem heard that Samaria had received the word of God, they sent Peter and John to them, 15 who, when they had come down, **prayed for them that they might receive the Holy Spirit**. 16 For as yet He had fallen upon none of them. They had only been baptized in the name of the Lord Jesus. 17 **Then they laid hands on them, and they received the Holy Spirit.***

ANOTHER WAY
Acts 9:17 *Another way is to be instructed directly by God*

ANOTHER FILLING

Acts 9:17 (NKJV) *And Ananias went his way and entered the house;* **and laying his hands on** *him he said, "Brother Saul, the Lord Jesus, who appeared to you on the road as you came, has sent me* **that you may receive your sight and be filled with the Holy Spirit."**

ANOTHER WAY

Acts 19:5-8 Laying on of hands to those who desire to reason and persuade others concerning the kingdom of God.

ANOTHER FILLING

Acts 19:5-8 (NKJV) *And when Paul had* **laid hands** *on them, the Holy Spirit came upon them, and they spoke with tongues and prophesied. 7 Now the men were about twelve in all. 8 And he went into the synagogue and spoke boldly for three months, reasoning and persuading concerning the things of the kingdom of God*

ANOTHER WAY

4. Through the seekers personal prayer and faith and asking **Luke 11:9 – 13; John 7:37 – 39**

ANOTHER FILLING

Luke 11:9-13 (NKJV) *"So I say to you, ask, and it will be given to you; seek, and you will find; knock, and it will be opened to you. 10 For everyone who asks receives, and he who seeks finds, and to him who knocks it will be opened. 11 If a son asks for bread from any father among you, will he give him a stone? Or if he asks for a fish, will he give him a serpent instead of a fish? 12 Or if he asks for an egg, will he offer him a scorpion? 13 If you then, being evil, know how to give good gifts to your children,* *how much more will your heavenly Father give the Holy Spirit to those who ask Him!"*

PREPARING FOR WHEN THE SPIRIT IS GIVEN

John 7:37-39 (NKJV) *On the last day, that great day of the feast, Jesus stood and cried out, saying, "If anyone thirsts, let him come to Me and drink. 38 He who believes in Me, as the Scripture has said, out of his heart will flow rivers of living water." 39 But this He spoke concerning the Spirit, whom those believing in Him would receive; for the Holy Spirit was not yet given, because Jesus was not yet glorified.*

A COMMAND

Eph 5:18 (NKJV) *And do not be drunk with wine, in which is dissipation;* *but be filled with the Spirit,*

I must reemphasize that this is a command and to put it in simple terms, don't get drunk, but be filled with God.

But be filled with the Spirit,
TRUE MEANING = BE BEING FILLED (CONTINUALLY FILLED), we have been filled to overflowing with the baptism of the Holy Spirit and now it is time to no longer dissipate but to continually be filled.

YOU WILL RECIEVE POWER TO WITNESS
Luke 4:17-19 (NKJV) *He found the place where it was written:*
18 "The Spirit of the Lord is upon Me,
Because He has anointed Me
To preach the gospel to the poor;
He has sent Me to heal the brokenhearted,
To proclaim liberty to the captives
And recovery of sight to the blind,
To set at liberty those who are oppressed;

19 To proclaim the acceptable year of the Lord."

THE WORD WITNESS IS ALSO THE WORD MARTYR
Stephen was a martyr and he was a witness

Acts 7:54-60 (NKJV) When they heard these things they were cut to the heart, and they gnashed at him with their teeth. 55 But he, being full of the Holy Spirit, gazed into heaven and saw the glory of God, and Jesus standing at the right hand of God, 56 and said, "Look! I see the heavens opened and the Son of Man standing at the right hand of God!" 57 Then they cried out with a loud voice, stopped their ears, and ran at him with one accord; 58 and they cast him out of the city and stoned him. And the witnesses laid down their clothes at the feet of a young man named Saul. 59 And they stoned Stephen as he was calling on God and saying, "Lord Jesus, receive my spirit." 60 Then he knelt down and cried out with a loud voice, "Lord, do not charge them with this sin." **And** when he had said this, he fell asleep.

Stephen was a true witness, and he was a true martyr for he was willing to give his life for the sake of the gospel and he did give his life for the sake of the gospel.

A martyr is one who gives his life for something. One who is willing to die for something. I have often heard it said you got to be willing to die for something or your living for nothing. When Stephen called these people stiffnecked people and proclaim the gospel they cast him out of the city and stoned him. The people who stoned him laid down their coats at Saul's feet, while Stephen was calling upon the Lord, and saying receive my spirit.

Romans 8:28 (KJV) says if you love God and are called according to his purpose all things were work together for good. For we know that Saul fell from his horse on the road to Damascus and was blinded. Not only was his name change from Saul to Paul but after Ananias laid hands on his eyes and he could once again see he became very zealous of works for the Lord..

All this to say death of the flesh has benefits for your works being a martyr, and a witness is a blessing.

YOU SHALL BE WITNESSES

Acts 1:8 (NKJV) But you shall receive power when the Holy Spirit has come upon you; and **you shall be witnesses** to Me in Jerusalem, and in all Judea and Samaria, and to the end of the earth."

After the Holy Spirit came upon Jesus, he was there with power as well as a witness. Paul said that he felt as if he was one born out of season he mentioned coming face-to-face with Jesus after Jesus's death burial and resurrection. Paul have to be prepared for the work that was ahead of him, so he had to be baptized in the Holy Spirit.

*WITNESS - **MARTUS** / One who presents facts based on their own authority. In the New Testament, witnessing of Jesus became the cause of death, therefore the Lord Jesus, in the book of Revelation chapter 15 is called the witness, the faithful one, this is derived from the word marturion, the definition being: on the declaration which confirms or something evidential, i.e. (genitive case) evidence given or (specially), the Decalogue (in the sacred Tabernacle):--to be testified, testimony, witness. This word is the word **from which you get the word martyr**. (MARTYR)*

The Holy Spirit was a witness in a new capacity as he descended upon Jesus after baptism. Jesus receive power, and the Holy Spirit with him witness all that he did. Once you receive the Holy Spirit through the baptism of the Holy Spirit you become a witness with power.

RECEIVE THE WITNESS

THE HOLY SPIRIT AS WITNESS

The Holy Spirit was there when Jesus laid his glory down

The Holy Spirit was there when Jesus was born of the virgin
The Holy Spirit was there when Jesus walked as a man
The Holy Spirit was there, and descended upon Jesus for power
The Holy Spirit was there, when Jesus began the miracles
The Holy Spirit was there when Jesus died on the cross
The Holy Spirit was there to raise Jesus from the dead
The Holy Spirit was there when Jesus ascended into heaven

RECEIVE THE BAPTISM OF THE HOLY SPIRIT AND YOU BECOME A WITNESS.

THE HOLY SPIRIT IS QUALIFIED TO MAKE YOU A WITNESS.

YOU KILL THE OLD MAN WITH THE ANOINTING OF THE HOLY SPIRIT AND THE WASHING AND REGENERATION OF THE WORD.

Killing the old man makes you a martyr, and a witness.

Romans 6:6-7 (KJV) Knowing this, that our old man is crucified with *him*, that the body of sin might be destroyed, that henceforth we should not serve sin. For he that is dead is freed from sin

THE HOLY SPIRIT'S RETURN
IN A DIFFERENT OPERATION
TO HELP YOU GET DRESSED
FOR THE WEDDING
John 14:15-16 (NKJV) And I will pray the Father, and He will give you another Helper, that He may abide with you forever--

THE HOLY SPIRIT MAKES YOU A WITNESS
He was there

Acts 1:8 (NKJV) But you shall receive power when the Holy Spirit has come upon you; **and you shall be witnesses** to Me in Jerusalem, and in all Judea and Samaria, and to the end of the earth."

NOW YOU ARE THE WITNESS

Matt 28:18-20 (NKJV) "All authority has been given to Me in heaven and on earth. 19 Go therefore and make disciples of all the nations, **baptizing them in the name of the Father and of the Son and of the Holy Spirit, 20 teaching them to observe all things that I have commanded you; and lo, I am with you always, even to the end of the age."** Amen.

CHRIST IS REVEALED TO THE BELEIVER BY THE HOLY SPIRIT

He shall glorify me: for he shall take of mine, and shall show it unto you. All things that the Father hath are mine.

Therefore I say that he shall take of mine, and shall show it unto you. John 16:14, 15. No one knows Jesus as the Holy Spirit does. He was the Christ through the eternities and throughout his earthly ministry, even to sacrifice on the cross as a servant of all, just as the servant of Abraham told Rebecca of the unknown and unseen bridegroom, Isaac in Genesis 24:33 – 36, so the Holy Spirit reveals the glories of the Christian's heavenly bridegroom.

THE HOLY SPIRIT WAS THERE

Jesus was conceived by the Holy Spirit
Luke 1:30 – 31, 34 – 35, Matthew 1:18 – 20
Jesus was baptized by the Holy Spirit
Matthew 3:16, Luke 4:1

Jesus was led by the Holy Spirit to be tempted in the wilderness
Matthew 4:1 – 2, Luke 4:1 – 2
Jesus performed all his mighty works by the Holy Spirit,
Acts 10:38
Jesus was anointed to preach by the Holy Spirit
Luke 4:18
Jesus died on the cross through the Holy Spirit
Hebrews 9:14
Jesus is raised from the dead by the Holy Spirit
1 Peter 3:18
Jesus gave his post-resurrection instructions to his apostles through
the Holy Spirit acts 1:1 – 2

DO YOU DESIRE TO COME AFTER JESUS?

Matt 16:24-25 (NKJV) Then Jesus said to His disciples, **"If anyone desires to come after Me, let him deny himself, and take up his cross, and follow Me.** 25 For whoever desires to save his life will lose it, but whoever loses his life for My sake will find it.

DENY YOURSELF

Luke 9:23-24 (NKJV) Jesus made a statement that if we desire to come after him, then we must deny ourselves, and take up his cross daily, and follow him. Remember Jesus went to the disciples and said follow me, and they dropped what they were doing and follow Jesus. They didn't desire to save their lives. They desire to lose their lives for his sake, because they knew that he was the Messiah.

THERE ARE TWO GARMENTS

CHITON = *The undergarment. It clothes you.*
STOLE = *Very descriptive outerwear, such as for a king, a priest, a ruler, royalty. No one has to describe you. The glory is seen in your outer wear.*

When you receive salvation you also receive righteousness, but you must keep your garment unspotted to avoid nakedness and Shane. Rev 16:15 (KJV) Behold, I come as a thief. Blessed *is* he that watcheth, and keepeth his garments, lest he walk naked, and they see his shame.

CLOTHED IN CHITON AND STOLE SALVATION AND RIGHTEOUSNESS

Isaiah 61:10 (NKJV) I will greatly rejoice in the Lord,
My soul shall be joyful in my God;

CLOTHED IN A GARMENT AND ROBED IN RIGHTEOUISNESS

For He has clothed me with the garments of salvation,
He has covered me with the robe of righteousness,

YOU ARE BLESSED, YOU ARE ROYALTY

Although the inner garment clothes your nakedness, the outer garment shows your position and and tells who you are. A magistrate would wear a certain garment, an ambassador would wear certain garment, a king would wear certain garment. You are royalty and you should expect the very best.

THE STOLE AND JEWELS SHOW WHO YOU ARE AS ROYALTY

As a bridegroom decks himself with ornaments,
And as a bride adorns herself with her jewels.

JESUS PURCHASED OUR OUTER WEAR AS WELL AS THE UNDERGARMENT. ALL YOU HAVE TO DO IS PUT IT ON, WITH THE HELP OF THE HOLY SPIRIT

Forsake not your fellowship

let us not forget the oil. We must make an effort to stay filled. We must keep our lamps filled so as to see our way to Christ, when the shout comes; THE BRIDEGROOM COMETH

Be like the wise virgins. Be filled with oil, be adorned and trimmed at the wick, and be ready.

WE MUST BE READY TO GO OUT AND MEET HIM!

A BRIDE FOR ABRAHAM'S SON

Gen 24:1-67

Abraham was an old man advanced in age and he was greatly blessed as God had promised him. Abraham had a great desire to see his son married, but had certain stipulations. Because he knew God, and his family knew God he wanted someone of his family and of God to marry, Isaac, so he made his servants where that he would not take a wife for his son from the daughters of the Canaanites.

JESUS BRIDE IS FROM THE HOUSEHOLD OF GOD AND FROM THE FAMILY OF GOD.

Eliezer expresses starts Abraham, and asked what this woman is not willing to follow me back to this land. What if she wants to see what Isaac looks like, what is see if they get along, or to see if they have anything in common. Do I have to take your son Isaac back for the woman to see him. Abraham said, no do not take my son back to see her it's God who took me from that land from my family and who spoke to me and swore to me saying to your descendents I give this land. He will send his Angels before you and you shall take a wife for my son from there and if the woman is not willing to follow you, then you are released from your old, but you must not take my son there. After that Eliezer swore the oath to Abraham.

Just as Abraham was unwilling for Isaac to go back to the land in which he(Abraham) came from, so God the father is not willing that His son

should go back to the earth before this union and marriage, that he go not back where the son was slain, and put through ridicule and torture.

*Then the servant took ten of his master's camels and departed, **for all his master's goods were in his hand.** And he arose and went to Mesopotamia, to the city of Nahor.*

Jesus offered the church through the Holy Spirit all that he had. He has trusted His massive inheritance to the hands of the Holy Spirit to be distributed to His bride, The Church.

Eliezer made his camels kneel down outside the city by a well of water in the evening, this is the time when women go out to draw water. Eliezer Then said, "O Lord God of my master Abraham, please give me success this day, and show kindness to my master Abraham. Here I stand by the well of water, and the daughters of the men of the city are coming out to draw water. Let it be that the young woman to whom I say, 'Please let down your pitcher that I may drink,' and she says, 'Drink, and I will also give your camels a drink' also let her be the one that you have appointed for Your servant Isaac. And by this I will know that You have shown kindness to my master."

Many are called but few are chosen. This is a true statement based on what you do when Jesus is offered to you. Are you willing to respond to his offer? and how will you respond to the one who holds all of the master's goods,(the Holy Spirit) We see that Rebecca was mature enough, and willing to serve the servant.

15 And it happened, before he had finished speaking, that behold, Rebekah, who was born to Bethuel, son of Milcah, the wife of Nahor, Abraham's brother, came out with her pitcher on her shoulder. 16 Now the young woman was very beautiful to behold, a virgin; no man had known her. And she went down to the well, filled her pitcher, and came up

A CHASTE VIRGIN TO CHRIST

2 Cor 11:1-2
Who has more of a right to be jealous than God. All things are his. He has betrothed us to one husband, and will present us as a chaste virgin to Christ.

NO SPOTS, NO WRINKLES

Eph 5:26-27
Jesus will present us to himself a glorious church not having spot, which I believe to be sin or wrinkles, which I believe to be faults, or blemishes, which I believe to be habits

Now the young woman was very beautiful to behold,

ZEALOUS OF GOOD WORKS

Titus 2:13-14
This Scripture says that Jesus gave himself to redeem us from every lawless deed. That means we can be the redeemed from every lawless deed. He also wished to purify us for himself and make us a very special people zealous of good works.

.And she went down to the well, filled her pitcher, and came up

QUALIFIED BRIDE REBECCA

Rebecca was qualified to be a bride because of her willingness to serve And the servant ran to meet her and said, "Please let me drink a little water from your pitcher." So she said, "Drink, my lord." Then she quickly let her pitcher down to her hand, and gave him a drink. And when she had finished giving him a drink, she said, "I will draw water for your camels also, until they have finished drinking.

"Then she quickly emptied her pitcher into the trough, ran back to the well to draw water, and drew for all his camels. And the man, wondering at her, remained silent so as to know whether the Lord had made his journey prosperous or not.

He also gave precious things to her brother and to her mother.

ABRAHAMS SERVANT IS A TYPE OF THE HOLY SPIRIT
REBEKAH REPRESENT THE BRIDE OF CHRIST
ISAAC IS A TYPE OF CHRIST

The servant traveled on a long journey to retrieve a kinsman for marriage. On his way back to his master, there was great joy when Rebecca saw her spouse.

The Holy Spirit has come into this country to receive kinsman of Christ. The Holy Spirit brought gifts, and fortunately those who are to go back with him served him with no coaxing, but out of a pure heart.

IF YOU WANT TO KNOW WHO IT IS COMING TO GREET US AS WE ARE RAPTURED, ASK THE HOLY SPIRIT

THE VEIL
The servant said, "It is my master." **So she took a veil and covered herself.**

*Rebecca **with veiled face** lit off of the camel and ran to receive the embrace of her husband.*

Rebecca's veil is to be discarded as she moves into a new and living way of life with Isaac her husband.

THE VEIL
Heb 10:19-20 says that we have the boldness to enter in to the holy of holies by the blood of Jesus, and we have a new living way which Jesus has consecrated for us through the veil that is to say his flesh.

We have communion with the blood, and his flesh. The blood is the only way that you can enter in to the holy of holies. The high priest could only enter into the holy of holies with blood to be sprinkled on the mercy seat. And this Scripture lets us know that the veil of Jesus is his flesh, which consecrates us into a new and living way.

I believe we will be changed

We will be caught up in the air to meet Jesus and as it says in first John 3:3 we do not know what will become but we know what we will be like him for we will see him as he is, and first Corinthians 15:51 we will not all sleep but we will be changed in a flash, in a twinkling of the eye at the last Trump goes on to say that mortality will put on immortality and corruption will put on incorruption. **I believe our veil or flesh will not only be disguarded, but transformed as we are caught up with the master.**

Gen 24:62-64 (KJV)

And Isaac came from the way of the well Lahairoi; for he dwelt in the south country. **63** And Isaac went out to meditate in the field at the eventide: and he lifted up his eyes, and saw, and, behold, the camels *were* coming. **64** And Rebekah lifted up her eyes, and when she saw Isaac, she lighted off the camel.

We'll meet him in the air
just as Rebecca jumped off of the camel and ran to meet her husband so shall we be caught up by the Holy Spirit to meet with Jesus in the air.

IT IS APPROPRIATE TO COVER WITH THE VEIL BEFORE MARRIAGE

66 And the servant told Isaac all the things that he had done. 67 Then Isaac brought her into his mother Sarah's tent; and he took Rebekah and she became his wife, and he loved her. So Isaac was comforted after his mother's death.

BECAUSE YOU KEPT MY COMMAND
THE CHURCH OF PHILADELPHIA

Rev 3:9-10
Here the Lord is speaking to the church of Philadelphia. Apparently this church leader and the people of the church were obedient to the word of God, and God's commandments with patience. The Lord said that they would be kept from the test that is to come upon the whole earth. I believe this is an indication that they will go in the rapture, because if the trial is to come upon the whole earth where would they hide.

WITHOUT HOLINESS NO MAN SHALL SEE GOD

Heb 12:13-14 (NKJV) *Pursue peace with all people, and holiness, without which no one will see the Lord.*

In this passage holiness is speaking of purity

PURE IS HOLY

Matt 5:8 (NKJV) *Blessed are the pure in heart, For they shall see God. If you're pure in heart you shall see God.*

LOOK FOR JESUS RETURN

Titus 2:13-14 (NKJV) *looking for the blessed hope and glorious appearing of our great God and Savior Jesus Christ,*

HOPE PURIFIES

1 John 3:2-3 (NKJV) Beloved, now we are children of God; and it has not yet been revealed what we shall be, but we know that when He is revealed, we shall be like Him, for we shall see Him as He is. **3 And everyone who has this hope in Him purifies himself, just as He is pure.**

LET ME END BY SAYING; YOU MUST BE FOUND WORTHY

Luke 21:36

says that we have to watch, and we have to pray. And the word of God says that we are to pray always that we may be found worthy to escape the things that are to come to pass in the earth. Notice the part that says: **may be found worthy.**

Stop looking for the tribulation in fear, and start looking for the rapture in hope.

FINALLY MY BROTHERS AND SISTERS
BUY YOUR OIL, OBEY JESUS' WORD, WALK IN THE SPIRIT,
LOOK FOR HIS RETURN, AND WATCH AND PRAY THAT
YOU BE FOUND WORTHY TO GO IN THE RAPTURE.

Are you going through relationship problems?
Are you depressed?
Do you need healing?
Are you unsure of your salvation?
Are you unsure if there's a heaven or hell?

Let me pray with you a prayer that is guaranteed for God to hear you.

PLEASE PRAY THIS PRAYER FROM YOUR HEART

Dear heavenly father I come before you a sinner.

I believe you sent your son to the earth to live for me, and to die for me, and raised from the dead for me, so that I can experience eternal life, and not hell. Thank you for bearing my sins, so that I don't have to. Come into my heart, and live through me, so that I may live for you. Thank you Lord for saving me.

If you prayed this prayer in faith, please direct correspondence to:

Heaven bound ministries
James H. Rayner
PO Box #235
6425 LEORNARDTOWN RD
BRYANTOWN, MD. 20617

Reflection

WHAT

Is

THE RAPTURE?

JEWISH CUSTOM

Are you willing to do what the Scripture says, so that you may go in the rapture?

During the Jewish wedding process the son chooses the bride, he then goes to negotiate with her father for her hand in marriage. After the negotiation is finished the bridegroom goes to his father to prepare a place for his bride. Normally this is a place built onto the house. This time. Takes at least a year, and during this time the bridegroom is not permitted to go to war, nor is he permitted to return for his bride until the father says it's time: Go Get Your Bride.

We must be the adorned church, to be the bride. Do you think all Christians are going to be the bride? And are you making yourself ready?

WHAT IS THE RAPTURE?

The rapture is the means by which Jesus will come for his bride.

The wedding table is set, the mansions are built, my question to you is are you dressed for the wedding.

The rapture is the means by which Father God sends Jesus for his bride.

WHAT ARE WE TO DO? <u>GET DRESSED!</u>

Matt 22:2-14

A certain King while making a marriage for his son sent his servants to bid people come to the wedding and they would not come, so he sent his servants out again to compel them to come to the wedding. When he came to see the wedding guests there was a man without a wedding garment on. He says to him: friend, why did you come without a wedding garment? The man was speechless. The King tells his servants to bind the man hand and foot, take him away and cast him into outer darkness where there will be weeping and gnashing of teeth. **This King's feels very passionate about this wedding.**

The bride will be ready, and shall be the wife.

Rev 19:7

This Scripture is showing that the wedding will not fail. Someone is going to marry the Christ. Someone will be the bride. Not all, because the bride makes herself ready, and everyone is not willing.

I ask again; what is the rapture? Look at what was said to the church of Philadelphia. The last of the seven churches in Revelation's.

Because you have kept my word

Rev 3:10-11 (KJV) Because thou hast kept the word of my patience, I also will keep thee from the hour of temptation, which shall come upon all the world, to try them that dwell upon the earth.

Because you have kept God's word of patience, he will keep you

*I answer the question. **The rapture is God the father's appointment of the son's return for his bride.** Just as Eliezer the servant went and brought*

Rebecca to Isaac in the field, so shall the Holy Spirit bring the bride of Jesus in the air to meet him in the rapture.

IT'S ALL ABOUT JESUS'S WEDDING.

As Christians we are living in the most exciting time throughout all history. We are living in the best of times, and yet, the worst of times. *The best of times because of; 1 Thess 4:16 which says the dead in Christ shall rise first and then those of us who remain shall be caught up to meet Jesus in the air; and the worst of times because of 2 Tim 3:1-13, Which says that perilous times shall come and men shall be lovers of themselves and then it expresses all of the evil in the hearts of men in the last days.*

Best of Times and Worst of Times

1 Thess 4:16-17
The Lord is coming out of heaven with a shout, and as the word says with the voice of an Archangel and with the Trump of God and the dead in Christ shall rise first. And then we which remain shall be caught up to meet him together in the air

*Surely this shall be the greatest time in all of history, *when the veil is pulled back and all of those of us in the second half of the book of Acts, step forward to take a bow ; not a bow for ourselves, or for any performance,* **but a bow before the King of Kings, and Lord of Lords who has come for his saints as promised.**

Worst of Times

2 Tim 3:1-13 (KJV)
Perilous times are dangerous times and as it says in **2 Tim 3:1-13 (KJV)** these times shall come. For men shall be lovers of their own selves, covetous, boasters, proud, blasphemers, disobedient to parents, unthankful, unholy, 3 Without natural affection, trucebreakers,

false accusers, incontinent, fierce, despisers of those that are good,
4 Traitors, heady, highminded, lovers of pleasures more than lovers
of God;

*it is not my purpose to explain all of 2 Tim 3:1-4 at this time, but only
what is beneficial for the study of this book and it's topic.*

Again

WHAT IS THE RAPTURE?

If you want to go in the rapture, this book is for you.

What is the rapture?

BEING CAUGHT UP

Rapture: *is the word Harpazo*

Harpazo means- to snatched out of dangers way.

*Although this word is not used in the greek translation, it is used in
the Latin Vulgate Bible, and recorded as rapture.

TO SNATCH OUT OF THE WAY OF DANGER. WHAT
DANGER?

I BELIEVE THE DANGER TO BE; THE TRIBULATION.

*Although a lot of action takes place in the book of revelations, **there are two
doctrines, that stand out;** truly as last day events. One that give people
great joy, and one that gives people great fear.*

They are the Rapture and the Tribulation.

WHAT IS THE TRIBULATION? IT IS THE DAY OF THE LORD!

The Day of the Lord

The day of final judgment

The day of the Lord shall be upon every one that is proud and lofty every one that is lifted up shall be brought low today by the Lord, with the wrath of God upon those who he will destroy.

The character of the day of the Lord

Isaiah 2:12
For the day of the LORD of hosts shall be upon every one that is proud and lofty, and upon every one that is lifted up; and he shall be brought low.

Isaiah 13:6
Wail, for the day of the LORD is at hand! It will come as destruction from the Almighty.

Isaiah 13:9
Behold, the day of the LORD comes,
Cruel, with both wrath and fierce anger,
To lay the land desolate;
And He will destroy its sinners from it.

THIS IS WHY THE RAPTURE MUST TAKE THE SAINTS OUT OF THE WAY OF DANGER

THE TWO EVENTS EXPECTED:

1. As aforementioned: **Rapture = Harpazo** *and*

IN THE LATIN VULGATE AS RAPTURE, BUT THE SPIRIT OF THE WORD IS IN THE KING JAMES VERSION. <u>AS CAUGHT UP.</u>

2. Tribulation *in Koine Greek =* **Phlipsis**
Phlipsis = tribulation, danger, oppression, persecution, tyranny, affliction. I believe each one of these things will be involved in the tribulation.

TO BE RAPTURED MEANS TO BE SNATCHED OUT OF HARMS WAY.

WHICH ONE ARE YOU LOOKING FOR?

To look for tribulation, is to look for it in Fear

Luke 21:25-28 says there will be signs in the sun, in the moon, and in the stars; and on the earth distress of nations, with perplexity, the sea and the waves roaring; **men's hearts failing them from fear and the expectation of those things which are coming on the earth,** for the powers of heaven will be shaken. Then they will see the Son of Man coming in a cloud with power and great glory. Now when these things begin to happen, look up and lift up your heads, because your redemption draws near."

Those who fear and expect those things which are coming upon the earth are the ones who will see the Son of Man coming in a cloud with great power and great glory. Look up because your redemption draws near.

To look for the Rapture, should be with Hope

Titus 2:11-15 (NKJV) For the grace of God that brings salvation has appeared to all men, 12 teaching us that, denying ungodliness and worldly lusts, we should live soberly, righteously, and godly in the present age, 13 looking for **the blessed hope and glorious appearing of our great God and Savior Jesus Christ, 14 who gave Himself**

for us, that He might redeem us from every lawless deed **and purify for Himself** His own special people, zealous for good works. 15 Speak these things, exhort, and rebuke with all authority. Let no one despise you.

THE HOPE THAT PURIFIES

1 JN 3:2

This passage of Scripture says that we do not know what we will become. This looks like we have a hope apply to our faith because we are putting our trust in the appearing of the Lord. The word of God says that we will be like him when we see him and we will see him as he is. This is why it's so important for us to apply our faith and to patiently wait with our hope for the return of Christ because the word also says that hope is what purifies us and make us pew or even as Jesus is pure.

TO BE PURE IS TO BE HOLY

HEB 12:14

We should follow peace with all men and holiness. Let them see your Holiness let them see your peace, because this is what's going to take you to the Lord.

It is a command for us to follow peace and holiness without which no man shall see the Lord. We know how to walk in peace but how do we walk in holiness? Well; we became righteousness because of the Jesus impartation of righteousness in us, now walk in righteousness and this will fulfill holiness. **Example:** *in a Jewish wedding betrothal, the bridegroom gives the keddussin (contract) and the mohar (dowery) to the father of the bride. Then the bridegroom goes to his fathers house to build onto it, for the bride and himself.* **It is up to the father to let the bridegroom know when it is time to go get his bride.**

JESUS IS THE SON WHO IS BUILDING ONTO THE HOUSE OF HIS FATHER, WHO HAS MANY MANSIONS. JESUS MUST AWAIT THE COMMAND OF THE FATHER TO RETURN FOR HIS BRIDE.

WHAT IS THE RAPTURE BASED ON?

TRADITIONAL JEWISH WEDDING

AND THE WORD OF GOD

JOHN'S PURPOSE WAS TO HELP JESUS GET DRESSED

FOR THE WEDDING

HELPING HIM TO PUT ON PROCLAMED RIGHTEOUSNESS

When John baptized Jesus, he was unworthy to do so as he stated, but who better to baptize our King, and Lord than the one who was baptized by the Holy Spirit in his mother's womb.

only John the Baptist.

* In a Jewish wedding, it was the job of the friend of the Bridegroom (also know as the best man). To help the bridegroom get dressed for the wedding.

FRIEND OF THE BRIDEGROOM

John 3:29-31 (KJV) 29 He that hath the bride is the bridegroom: but the friend of the bridegroom, which standeth and heareth him, rejoiceth greatly because of the bridegroom's voice: this my joy therefore is fulfilled. **30** He must increase, but I *must* decrease. **31** He that cometh from above is above all: he that is of the earth is earthly, and speaketh of the earth: he that cometh from heaven is above all. *We take the tradition of having a best man for the bridegroom, from the Jewish wedding.*

After the wedding in heaven, John the Baptist will be standing at the door of the hupah (bridechamber), to hear the voice of the Lord, and this will bring him great joy because his purpose will of been fulfilled.

JESUS PAID FOR OUR WEDDING GARMENTS

Isaiah 61:10 (NKJV) will greatly rejoice in the Lord,
My soul shall be joyful in my God;
For He has clothed me with **the garments of salvation,**
He has covered me with **the robe of righteousness,**
As a bridegroom decks himself with ornaments,
And as a bride adorns herself with her jewels.

I believe John's greatness was contributed to the fact that he was **filled with the Holy Spirit** *to prepare the way for Jesus.*

NOT A MAN GREATER EXCEPT THE LEAST IN CHRIST

Matt 11:11
This Scripture is saying that among men there has not been born a greater man among women, but more than that is says there has not risen a greater than John the Baptist. When he speaks of risen it speaks of his purpose and his calling. Truly we can talk about Moses, we can talk about Elijah, we can even talk about Enoch, and even David or Solomon. Out of all these mentioned great man that was non-that had a greater calling for purpose than John the Baptist. Notice the Scripture continues to say that the least in the kingdom of heaven is greater than he. John the Baptist was prepared to prepare

the way for Jesus's first coming, so therefore he was filled with the Holy Ghost from his mothers womb. As the church it is mentioned that the least in the kingdom of heaven is greater than he. Keep in mind that the kingdom of heaven receive the Holy Spirit and are witnesses when we minister and help others to enter the kingdom of heaven. We are here to minister Jesus's second coming.

ARE YOU IN THE KINGDOM OF HEAVEN? IF YOU ARE, YOU ARE ONE OF THOSE THAT IS THE GREATER THAN JOHN THE BAPTIST
IN PURPOSE AND POSITION WITH CHRIST.

The Holy Spirit had to use a man.(after all, Heaven and earth are to be united).

JESUS SAID: YOU ARE RIGHT, BUT ALLOW ME TO GET DRESSED FOR MY WEDDING

Matt 3:14-15
Even though John was unworthy to help Jesus get dressed,

Jesus allowed it for your sake and mine, and for the sake of the wedding. Someone had to fit the role as a friend of the bridegroom in this Jewish wedding. Who better than the one who was totally sold out, and not mingling with the world it all, but the voice in the wilderness saying make straight your paths. He will also be the one who stands at the bridechamber (Hupah) in heaven and rejoice at the voice of the bridegroom. Jesus was saying in so many words when he said allowed to be so that all righteousness be fulfilled. Jesus was saying okay friend of the bridegroom were best man, help me to get dressed.(In my righteousness).

John was filled with the Holy Ghost to prepare for Jesus coming John 1:27

John spoke with the one who is coming after him, and who is preferred before him. He spoke rightly when he said she latches I'm not worthy to unloose. Notice he speaking of clothing either dressing or undressing. He speaks of clothing because it is the job of the bridegroom's best man to help them get dressed for the wedding.

Luke 1:41 When Elizabeth heard about Mary; Jesus 's mother, the baby leaped in her womb; she was filled with the Holy Spirit.

Luke 1:42-44 (KJV) And she said, Blessed art thou among women, and blessed is the fruit of thy womb. And whence is this to me, that the mother of my Lord should come to me? For, lo, as soon as the voice of thy salutation sounded in mine ears, the babe leaped in my womb for joy. Notice the baby leaped for joy. I present, that the baby leaped for joy even though it was not yet born from the womb of its mother, it leaped because it was also filled with the Holy Spirit.

A FATHER HAS JOY IN HIS SON GETTING MARRIED

THOU ART MY BELOVED SON, IN WHOM I AM WELL PLEASED

Mark 1:9-11 *Jesus came from Nazareth of Galilee, and after he was baptized by John the Baptist in the Jordan he came straightway up out of the water and saw the heavens open. Spirit like a dove descending upon him and a voice came from heaven that said; thou art my beloved son in whom I am well pleased.*

*Jesus was baptised. This was the righteousness being fulfilled he spoke of. John helped him get dressed for his wedding.He was wedding concious. Notice he went to a wedding immediately after.

Remember when he said; my time is not yet.He was talking about his wedding.

A GOOD THING

Prov 18:22 (NKJV) He who finds a wife finds a good thing,

And obtains favor from the Lord.

Jesus not only found a wife in the church, but he created the church. Although God the father is well pleased with his dearly beloved son I believe Jesus will receive even more honor and favor from the father, and the kingdom of heaven.

The Bride had to be of age or matured.

Song 8:8 (KJV) – we must teach her

We have a little sister, and she **hath no breasts**: what shall we do for our sister in the day when she shall be spoken for?

This passage of Scripture is using the breasts; as a metaphor for immaturity, and the lack of being prepared or adorned in the time that she is spoken for. We can also equate this passage with the church, because the song of Solomon is truly a love letter. The conclusion is come to which expresses our concern and our solution. Our solution is to teach the immature so that they will be ready to give their hand in marriage.

1 Cor 14:19-20 (KJV) – we must be mature

Brethren, be not children in understanding: howbeit in malice be ye children, but in understanding be men.

Even in the New Testament it is stated that we should be mature. In many passages that explains that we should be serious about the things of God therefore mature in our understanding. I personally know children with a much better understanding of the word of God than many adults.

There is an inheritance that awaits you

1 Peter 1:4 (KJV) an inheritance undefiled

The character of our inheritance is that it is incorruptible, and undefiled, and that fadeth not away, reserved in heaven for you

The Holy Spirit – A guarantee of our inheritance
Eph 1:11-14 (KJV)

In whom also we have obtained an inheritance, being predestinated according to the purpose of him who worketh all things after the counsel of his own will: That we should be to the praise of his glory, who first trusted in Christ. In whom ye also *trusted*, after that ye heard the word of truth, the gospel of your salvation: in whom also after that ye believed, ye were sealed with that holy Spirit of promise, **Which is the earnest of our inheritance until the redemption of the purchased possession,** unto the praise of his glory.

RIGHTEOUS = DIKAIOSUNE / Rather than to accept his own standard, or the standard of the law, man can submit to Gods standard of righteousness and accept his claim by faith allowing him the ability to stand in God's presence without guilt or shame.

YOU MUST BE PURE TO BE IN GODS PRESENCE

Eph 5:25-27

Jesus's desire was to make us his and at the same time cleanse us and make us pure. His desire was to present us to himself with his glorious nature which is honored in heaven. No sin, faults, or habits, of the earth, but purity.

2 Cor 5:21

Jesus was holy, and he knew no sin, but yet he took sin upon himself and even became sin because of our sinful nature which he took upon himself. Because of his righteousness and his righteous nature we became righteousness because of the exchange through the covenant between man and God.

RECIEVE AND GET THE POWER TO BECOME

John 1:12

*As you received him you are given the power to become a child of God, and therefore can mature to become a son of God. As a child of God you have now been given the power to become a son of God.

HOW TO BECOME A SON OF GOD

Teknon = Child of God

You are righteous as a child of God (you have the ability to stand in the presence of God without guilt and without shame.

Hagios = Son of God

as a son of God you have matured from righteousness to holiness. You have put on the outer garment that tells who you are.

THE HEIR

Gal 4:1-7

A child of God who happens to be an air has the same position as a servant even though he's master of everything, but because of his immaturity he must be under guardians and stewards until the father of points him as of being of age to receive his inheritance. Gal 4:1-7 says that when we were children, we were in bondage under the elements of the world. But a time came when God sent forth his son born of a woman born under the law to redeem those who were under the law that we might receive the adoption as sons. And because we are sons we have the spirit of sons in our hearts and we cry Abba which means our father. Our status is changed we no longer walk in the status of a servant but as the heir of God through Christ.

BECOMING A SON

A CHILD HAS THE SAME AUTHORITY AS A SERVANT UNTIL HE BECOMES OF FULL AGE (maturity)

HE IS UNDER TUTORS AND GOVENORS UNTIL HE IS OF FULL AGE

A CHILD DOESN'T UNDERSTAND OR HAVE THE ABILITY TO OBTAIN HIS INHERITANCE. HIS BONDAGE IS UNDER THE ELEMENTS OF THIS WORLD.

<u>YOU CAN MATURE TO WALK ABOVE THE STORM</u>

<u>AS A SON YOU CAN EVEN COMMAND THE STORM</u>

LIVE SOBERLY, RIGHTEOUSLY, AND GODLY

Titus 2:11-14

The grace of God, which meaning is God giving us will we don't deserve. It is through this grace that God has given salvation to all men, and this grace teaches us that by denying ungodliness and worldly lusts, we should live soberly righteously and godly, in this present world. We also learned that through this grace we should be looking for the blessed hope which is the appearing of our great God and our Savior Jesus Christ. He gave himself for us that he might redeem us from iniquity and purify us and to himself a peculiar people zealous of good works.

THIS IS GROWING UP IN GOD

CALL ON THE LORD OUT OF A PURE HEART

2 Tim 2:22 (KJV) Flee also youthful lusts: but follow righteousness, faith, charity, peace, with them that call on the Lord **out of a pure heart.**

Notice after we flee youthful lusts; we follow righteousness, faith, charity, peace, and we also follow them that call upon the name of the Lord out of a pure heart. That means we must follow holy people.

BECOMING HOLY, OR MATURE IN CHRIST

THE **HOPE** OF THE RAPTURE IS THE PURIFIER

TO BE PURE IS TO BE HOLY

Matt 5:8 (KJV) Blessed are the **pure in heart**: for **they shall see God.**

Heb 12:14 (KJV) Follow peace with all men, **and holiness, without which no man shall see the Lord:**

DO YOU SEE THE CONNECTION?

EVERYONE WHO HAS THIS HOPE

1 John 3:2-3
When we see Jesus we shall be transformed into what we shall be for eternity. And the word of God says that we will be like him for we shall see him as he is. One of the qualifiers is that we must have this hope in our hearts that we may be purified

WHAT IS THE RAPTURE?

WE HAVE TWO GARMENTS

What will you do with your garments?

YOU MUST BE INCORRUPTIBLE IN YOUR UNDERGARMENT AND ALSO DRESSED WITH YOUR OUTERGARMENT.

YOU CANNOT HAVE ON FILTHY UNDERCLOTHES AND NO OVERCLOTHES. Keep those undergarments unspotted unwrinkled and unblemished. When in a fault, just confess.

YOUR GARMENT CAN BE SPOTTED BY THE FLESH

Jude 1:21-23 (KJV) Keep yourselves in the love of God, looking for the mercy of our Lord Jesus Christ unto eternal life. 22 And of some have compassion, making a difference: 23 And others save with fear, pulling them out of the fire; **hating even the garment spotted by the flesh.**

Rev 16:15 Behold, I come as a thief. Blessed *is* he that watcheth, and keepeth his garments, lest he walk naked, and they see his shame.

Then don't walk in the flesh

1 John 1:9 (KJV)
if we have sinned, all we have to do is confess our sins. The word didn't even say to repent, just acknowledge that you have sinned and confess it. he is faithful and just to forgive us our sins, and to cleanse us from all unrighteousness

Mortify or put to death the deeds of the flesh

Romans 8:13
Just like this flesh will die one day, if we live after the flesh we will die spiritually, but we walk in the spirit which is eternal we shall live. This is speaking of the spirit of God that is within you.

Stop calling God a liar
we have sinned more than we realize

1 John 1:8-10 Don't say we have no sin confessed the sins that you know and request God to forgive you for those that you do not know. God is faithful and he's just and he will forgive us our sins he said he would. He said he would put our sins as far as the east is from the West. He said that he will throw with them into the sea of forgetfulness and remember them no more, and then he will cleanse us from all unrighteousness. If we say we have no sin his word is not in us

HATING THE SPOTTED GARMENT

Jude 1:23
This passage of Scripture is stating that some people will be saved by you telling them about the love of Jesus loved him and died for them on the cross, but there is a certain percentage who will only be saved through the fear and it is our job to show them love enough to pull them out of the fire even though we hate the fleshly deeds that they've done. I heard a well-known man of God see one time 80% will be saved by the love of Jesus, but another 20% will be saved by the fear of hell.

* By hating the spotted garment defiled by the flesh we are compelled to righteousness. Compelled to put away sin.

God says that he hates sin. He also says that because you have hated sin and loved righteousness therefore God has set you above your companions by anointing you with the oil of Joy and your robes are fragrant with myrrh and aloes and cassia; from Palaces adorned with ivory, the music of the strings makes you glad daughters of Kings are among your Honored women at your right hand is the Royal bride in gold of Ophir.

EPH 5:26 The Lord wants to wash and cleanse his church. He wants to sanctify it. To sanctify it means to separated into himself.

James 1:21 James says to lay aside all filthiness and superfluity of naughtiness.

The engrafted word of God is the word that becomes a part of you the only way to make the word a part of you is to actually apply it to your life. When you do the word and it becomes and is engrafted into you just like a plant that is engrafted into another plant. It is this word only that is able to save your soul.

CHITON - THE UNDERGARMENT

You have got to hate the spotted garment to get it clean. It is the garment that is closest to the flesh, but the undergarment must be clean.

THE OVERGARMENT MAKES YOU APROPRIATE FOR THE WEDDING, BECAUSE IT TELLS PEOPLE WHO YOU ARE.

Jesus didn't have to clean his undergarment because it was already clean.

FILTHY RAGS, BEFORE OUR RIGHTEOUSNESS

Isaiah 64:5-6 (KJV) you meet him that rejoice and work righteousness, those that remember you in your ways: you are angry; for we have sinned: in those is continuance, **and we shall be saved.**

Stop looking at my Sin; I know that I am a wretch, but so are you. We all are as unclean, and our righteousnesses filthy rags. We have no glory except that which is taken away by the wind because we fade as a leaf to stop pointing your finger at me and point your finger at you. JESUS UNDERGARMENT ALREADY UNSPOTTED. ALL HE HAD TO DO WAS PUT ON <u>HIS STOLE; (HIS RIGHTEOUS ROBE.)</u>

<u>He was already clean and incorruptible. He was the unspotted lamb. That unspotted sacrifice. The lamb of God that taketh away the sins of the world.</u>

<u>Jesus was salvation. Jesus was the undergarment but he is also the overgarment. He is salvation, but he is also righteousness.</u>

<u>AS A MAN HE WAS SALVATION (the last Adam)</u>

<u>THE GOSPELS</u>
<u>Matthew saw Jesus as a king</u>
<u>Mark saw Jesus as a great servant</u>
<u>Luke saw Jesus as a righteous man</u>
<u>John saw Jesus as God</u>

<u>John the Baptist baptized Jesus, so that the Holy Spirit would clothe him with the outer garment for the wedding. The garment of righteousness</u>

JESUS PAID FOR OUR WEDDING GARMENTS

Isaiah 61:10 (NKJV) will greatly rejoice in the Lord,
My soul shall be joyful in my God;
For He has clothed me with **the garments of salvation,**
He has covered me with **the robe of righteousness,**

As a bridegroom decks himself with ornaments,
And as a bride adorns herself with her jewels.

Acts 4:12 (KJV) Jesus came with the garments of salvation
Neither is there salvation in any other: for there is none other name
under heaven given among men, whereby we must be saved.

John 12:28 (KJV)
Father, glorify thy name. Then came there a voice from heaven,
saying, I have both glorified *it*, and will glorify *it* again.

*Jesus will be glorified again, and on the day of the wedding. The glorious
wedding.*

**Jesus did not have to put on the undergarment that can become spotted
with sin, because he knew no sin.*

*All he had to do was put on the outer garment, the wedding garment, the
stole which is the garment that tells who you are or the character of your
event.*

JESUS DIDN'T EVEN KNOW SIN

2 Cor 5:21 (KJV) For he hath made him to be sin for us, who knew
no sin; that we might be made the righteousness of God in him.
Jesus didn't even know sin until he encountered my sin, and your sin,
which was placed upon himself on the cross. And he did it to make
an uneven exchange.

LAMB OF GOD

John 1:29 (KJV) John the Baptist immediately recognize Jesus and
said: Behold the Lamb of God, which taketh away the sin of the
world.

THE WEDDING GARMENT = STOLE / This garment is representative of who you are. A ruler, royalty, commander, king, priest, or a person of high distinction. <u>IN OUR CASE AND THE GREATEST CASE</u> **THE BRIDE OF CHRIST**

This garment is an outer garment and is long and draped around the shoulders. Take note that it is the outer garment, and cannot be mistakened. WE ARE **ROYALTY**

UNDERGARMENT = CHITON / Jude 1:23 (KJV) And others save with fear, pulling them out of the fire; hating even the garment spotted by the flesh. **Some christians will stay in sin, right till the end. Christians hate sin even when they are waddling in it.**

<u>**You must know you do not have to have a spotted garment you can walk in righteousness, and you can keep your garment.**</u>

Eccl 9:8-9 (KJV)
When the benefits of keeping your garments always white is that healing comes quickly and you live a joyful life with your wife with two God has given to you and he says in his passion that that is your portion in life. In other words that's your blessing and favor from God.

Rev 16:15 (KJV)
When Jesus mentioned that he comes as a thief in the night, he also mentions that we should continue to watch keep our garments clean and as I have already mentioned an eccl 9:8 – 9 there are some blessings that come with keeping your garment white in this life as well as the next, and you will not be caught naked, and other see your shame.

DON'T TURN, GET DRESSED

2 Peter 2:21-22
It is better for you not to a known the way of righteousness into and turned from the righteous way and returned back to the world as a dog to his own vomit, or a washed peak back to waddling in the mud.

BE HOLY

For it would have been better for them not to have known the way of righteousness, than having known it, **to turn from the holy commandment**

UNDERGARMENT = CHITON / Jude 1:23 (KJV) And others save with fear, pulling them out of the fire; **hating even the garment spotted by the flesh.**

Don't spot your garment of salvation with sin. You have the spirit of the Lord, and cause condemnation or conflict with your spirit and soul.

Some Christians will stay in sin, right till the end. Christians hate sin even when they are waddling in it.

hating even the garment **spotted**
This word hate is the word **miseo** / a violent dislike of something. We should have a radically violent aversion to sin.

Heb 1:8-11 (NKJV) But to the Son He says:
"Your throne, O God, is forever and ever;
A scepter of righteousness is the scepter of Your Kingdom.
**9 You have loved righteousness and hated lawlessness;
Therefore God, Your God, has anointed You
With the oil of gladness more than Your companions."**

10 And: "You, Lord, in the beginning laid the foundation of the earth, And the heavens are the work of Your hands.
11 They will perish, but You remain;
And they will all grow old like a garment

Psalms 45:7-10 (NKJV)
You love righteousness and hate wickedness;
Therefore God, Your God, has anointed You
With the oil of gladness more than Your companions.
8 All Your garments are scented with myrrh and aloes and cassia,
Out of the ivory palaces, by which they have made You glad.
9 Kings' daughters are among Your honorable women;
At Your right hand stands the queen in gold from Ophir.
10 Listen, O daughter, Consider and incline your ear;
Forget your own people also, and your father's house;

Don't be caught naked
SPOTTED = SPILOS / To defile, contaminate. we must deal with these undergarment problems before they contaminate the outer garment. Ask the Lord what to deal with and how.

Rev 16:15 (KJV)
Behold, I come as a thief. Blessed *is* he that watcheth, and keepeth his garments, lest he walk naked, and they see his shame.

HIS WIFE HAS MADE HERSELF READY

SHE HAS TO BE MADE READY

Rev 19:7-9 (NKJV) Let us be glad and rejoice and give Him glory, **for the marriage of the Lamb has come, and His wife has made herself ready."** 8 And to her it was granted to be arrayed in fine linen, clean and bright, for the fine linen is the righteous acts of the saints.
9 Then he said to me, "Write: 'Blessed are those who are called to the marriage supper of the Lamb!'

The rapture gives us an urgency as the bride of Christ to prepare and to make ourselves ready for the wedding which is to take place in heaven during the tribulation.

ALRIGHT, IT'S TIME.

GO AND GET YOUR BRIDE

THE BRIDEGROOM LEAVES, AND RETURNS to HIS SERVANTS

IN THE EARTH

MK 13:34 For the Son of man is as a man taking a far journey, who left his house, and **gave authority to his servants,** and to every man his work, and commanded the porter to watch. [35] Watch ye therefore: for ye know not when the master of the house cometh, at even, or at midnight, or at the cockcrowing, or in the morning:

*PARABLE: Jesus is as a man taking a far journey, He left his house here in the earth with us (you and me, his servants). He gave us in the body of Christ, all something to do until his return. He also commanded his leaders, (the porters), to watch over his house, (the church). We know not when the master is to return.

CHURCH = ecclesia / THE church is an organism, not an organization. It is not limited to denomination; you can find it everywhere, it is without walls.

JESUS TOOK A JOURNEY, BUT WILL RETURN

*For the Son of man is **as a man taking a far journey,** who left his house,

John 14:1-3 (NKJV) In My Father's house are many mansions; if it were not so, I would have told you. **I go to prepare a place for you.** 3

And if I go and prepare a place for you, I will come again and receive you to Myself; that where I am, there you may be also.

HE LEFT TO PREPARE A PLACE FOR US, HIS SERVANTS
*Jesus has left to prepare a place for you and me. In the father's house there are many mansions for you and for me.

We are the bride. (The Church) **THOSE MATURE ENOUGH TO LOOK FOR HIM.**

Luke 21:36 (KJV) Watch ye therefore, and pray always, that ye **may be accounted worthy to escape** all these things that shall come to pass, and to stand before the Son of man.

*REMEMBER RAPTURE MEANS /
TO BE SNATCHED OUT OF THE WAY OF DANGER

THE RAPTURE IS JESUS RETURNING

FOR HIS BRIDE

NO SPOTS, NO WRINKLES (NO SIN)

Eph 5:25-27 (KJV) Husbands, love your wives, even as Christ also loved the church, and gave himself for it; **26** That he might sanctify and cleanse it with the washing of water by the word, **27 That he might present it to himself a glorious church, not having spot, or wrinkle, or any such thing**; but that it should be holy and without blemish.

JESUS WANTS TO MAKE YOU PURE AS HE IS. HE KNEW NO SIN BUT BECAME SIN AND PUT YOUR SIN AWAY, <u>SO YOU CAN BECOME LIKE HIM, PURE AND HOLY.</u>

LOVE NOT THE WORLD

1 John 2:14-15 (KJV) I have written unto you, fathers, because ye have known him that is from the beginning. I have written unto you, young men, because ye are strong, and the word of God abideth in you, and ye have overcome the wicked one. **15 Love not the world, neither the things that are in the world.** If any man love the world, the love of the Father is not in him.

WE; THE CHURCH ARE JOINED TO CHRIST

Eph 5:29-33 (KJV) For no man ever yet hated his own flesh; but nourisheth and cherisheth it, even as the Lord the church: **30 For we are members of his body, of his flesh, and of his bones. 31** For this cause shall a man leave his father and mother, **and shall be joined unto his wife, and they two shall be one flesh. 32** This is a great mystery: **but I speak concerning Christ and the church.**

*and gave **authority** to his servants, and to every man **his work**, and commanded the porter to watch.

PORTER - a porter is one employed to carry a load. THESE ARE THE LEADERS IN THE HOUSE (the church). This person must also be attentive and watch for the master's return.

TWO KINGDOMS

For man to have a realization of his existence he must do one of two things. He must build up, or tear down. Most men like the Donald Trumps, the Jay-Z's, and women such as Oprah Winfrey. are people who desire to leave a legacy behind, by building. They make something and grow it. There are however other people who either because of their background or failure to have a good self-image feel they can never attain to construct such a great legacy, so instead of building up or supporting others who do they are destructive, and attempt to tear down the works of others. Let us look at those who want to build.

Man has a great desire to build and that is a good thing, even a great thing, but once you meet Jesus the rules change. Either your desire is to build in the earth or your desire is to be obedient to God and build in heaven. God said he would add to you. He said he would do the building for you. **Jesus said to put your treasures in heaven. He asked you to trust him. He said that if any desire to be his disciples, they need to deny themselves, pick up their crosses and follow him.**

There is no other way to look at it than to see that you have a choice between two kingdoms. **A kingdom in the earth, or kingdom in heaven.**

I would never say that you would not make heaven, but where's your investment? Where is your treasures in heaven. Did you put any in heaven? A prayer, or a smile, a kind word. Did you lead someone into the kingdom?

Heavenly investment

Matt 6:19-20 (KJV)

you have a choice, where moth and rust corrupts it, and where thieves break through and steal it or you can lay it in heaven. This is the same offer that Jesus gave to the rich young ruler, and he could not do it but walked away.

DO YOU HAVE RICHES OR DO THEY HAVE YOU

Jesus showed a rich man how to inherit eternal life and told His disciples the danger of trusting riches

Mark 10:17–31 (KJV) And when he was gone forth into the way, there came one running, and kneeled to him, and asked him, Good Master, what shall I do that I may inherit eternal life? 18 And Jesus said unto him, Why callest thou me good? there is none good but one, that is, God. 19 Thou knowest the commandments, Do not commit adultery, Do not kill, Do not steal, Do not bear false witness, Defraud not, Honour thy father and mother. 20 And he answered and said unto him, Master, all these have I observed from my youth. **21 Then Jesus beholding him loved him, and said unto him, One thing thou lackest: go thy way, sell whatsoever thou hast, and give to the poor, and thou shalt have treasure in heaven: and come, take up the cross, and follow me. 22 And he was sad at that saying, and went away grieved: for he had great possessions.**

THIS WAS A MATTER OF INVESTING IN HEAVEN. I HEARD A PREACHER SAY THAT HE'S NOT GOING TO BE BROKE WHEN HE GETS TO HEAVEN AND SO HE WILL CONTINUE TO HOARD MONEY, AND PLACE IT IN THE BANKS.

He is very Wealthy materially, and it appears he's confusing his material wealth with spiritual wealth.

THAT'S A MATTER OF PERSPECTIVE
JESUS SAID GIVE TO THE POOR. THIS IN ITSELF IS AN INVESTMENT, BUT NOT FOR THE MAN DECEIVED BY MATERIAL WEALTH
*THIS IS HARD TO FOLLOW WHEN RICHES HAVE YOU

GOD WILL PAY AGAIN

Prov 19:17 (KJV) *He that hath pity upon the poor lendeth unto the LORD;* **and that which he hath given will he pay him again.**

WHY TALK ABOUT MONEY?

The kingdom of heaven is not food and drink

BECAUSE IN THE LAST 30 - 40 YEARS THE GOSPEL INTEREST APPEARS TO BE MONEY AND NOT THE LORD

Why do we talk about money when we are to be talking about the rapture?

Because you may have to choose between your earthly kingdom and the heavenly kingdom, where the rapture is to take you.

THE LOVE OF THE FATHER IS NOT IN HIM

1 John 2:14-15 this Scripture expresses that the the love of the father is not in those who love the world. I have written unto you, fathers, because ye have known him that is from the beginning. I have written unto you, young men, because ye are strong, and the word of God abideth in you, and ye have overcome the wicked one. **15 Love not the world, neither the things _that are_ in the world. If any man love the world, the love of the Father is not in him**

Well we need to **talk about the kingdom of God**, if that's where we are going.

HEAVEN'S WALL STREET

Matt 6:19-21 wherever your treasure is that is where your heart will be. Is your treasure in that Lamborghini, or Maserati, or 12 bedroom home? Something can very easily happened to these things. They can be stolen or destroyed, But lay up for yourselves treasures in heaven, where neither moth nor rust doth corrupt, and where thieves do not break through nor steal.

EARTHS KINGDOM

If you have enough money, _you've probably already built your kingdom here on the earth. So we need to talk about both kingdoms._

DON'T PUT YOURSELF IN POSITION TO HAVE TO CHOOSE BETWEEN HEAVEN'S KINGDOM AND EARTH'S KINGDOM

DON'T GET ME WRONG. GOD SAID, THAT YOU CAN HAVE WEALTH. NOTICE THAT THE BIBLE SAYS THAT JESUS LOVED THE RICH YOUNG RULER AS HE WALKED AWAY. AND ONE OF THE DISCIPLES SAID; HOW CAN ANY OF US BE SAVED?

YOU CAN BE RICH IN BOTH EARTH AND HEAVEN?

Matt 19:24-26 (KJV) When his disciples heard it, they were exceedingly amazed, saying, **Who then can be saved?** But Jesus beheld them, and said unto them, With men this is impossible; but with God all things are possible.

THE RICH MAN, AND LAZARUS, THE BEGGAR

Luke 16:19-31

There was a rich man, finely dressed, and who ate well. And even while he ate well there was a beggar named Lazarus who laid at his gate, and was full of sores. All he wanted was the crumbs that fell from the rich man's table of the dogs came and licked his sores. When the Lazarus the beggar died and was carried by the Angels to Abraham's bosom: the rich man also died and was buried; and in hell he lifted his eyes, being in torments and he saw Abraham afar off and Lazarus in his bosom and he cried Abraham, have mercy on me, send Lazarus that he may dip the tip of his finger in water and cool my tongue for I am tormented in this flame.

But Abraham said: son, remember during your lifetime you receive all good things, and likewise Lazarus only the evil things, but now he is comforted and you are tormented. And besides all of this there is a great Gulf and we can't get over there and you cannot get over here. The men said will immediately send it to my father's house I have five brothers and I don't want them come in here. Abraham said they had Moses to tell and the prophets let them hear them and he said if they don't hear Moses and the prophets/they listen to me, though one raised from the dead.

<u>Remember that thou in thy lifetime receivedst thy good things, and likewise Lazarus evil things: but now he is comforted, and thou art tormented.</u>

NOTICE TO BE RICH AND SAVED TOO, THERE ARE BIBLICAL PRINCIPALS AND GUIDELINES.

NOTICE: Lazarus ate the crumbs from the rich man's table. The rich man had no regard for the poor. If he had welcomed Lazarus to his table, and made an investment in how he treated him, he may not have ended up in hell.

We have many of the rich and famous of whom I commend, because they know right from wrong and try to bless those who are less forunate than they, but one thing they lack. SALVATION THROUGH THE BLOOD OF JESUS.

IF YOU ARE ONE OF THOSE, LET ME PRAY WITH YOU. BOW YOUR HEAD AND REPEAT AFTER ME;

Dear heavenly Father; I come to you, a sinner. I need forgiveness, and am willing to turn from sin. Thank you for sending your son who loved me, and shed his precious and innocent blood for me. Lord I invite you to come into my heart as my personal savior so that I may live for you, and the money I give now has meaning. Thank you Lord for saving me.

THERE IS ANOTHER GROUP, WHO ARE SAVED AND TEACH THE MONEY GOSPEL, AND NOT ALL, BUT SOME

HAVE ERRED BECAUSE OF THE LOVE OF MONEY AND ARE COVETEOUS. **_YOU NEED TO REPENT AND STOP BELIEVING THAT GAIN IS GODLINESS_**.

THERE ARE GUIDELINES FOR BEING RICH

AND BEING IN THE LORD

1 Tim 6:16-21 (KJV) Who only hath immortality, dwelling in the light which no man can approach unto; whom no man hath seen, nor can see: to whom be honour and power everlasting. Amen. **17 Charge them that are rich in this world, that they be not highminded, nor trust in uncertain riches, but in the living God, who giveth us richly all things to enjoy; 18 That they do good, that they be rich in good works, ready to distribute, willing to communicate; 19 Laying up in store for themselves a good foundation against the time to come, that they may lay hold on eternal life.** 20 O Timothy, keep that which is committed to thy trust, avoiding profane and vain babblings, and oppositions of science falsely so called: 21 Which some professing have erred concerning the faith. Grace be with thee. Amen.

BE NOT HIGHMINDED

DON'T TRUST YOUR RICHES

TRUST IN GOD

DO GOOD

BE RICH IN GOOD WORKS

READY TO DISTRIBUTE

THIS GIVES A GOOD FOUNDATION AGAINST THE TIME TO COME.

NOT JUST MONEY

ABUNDANT LIFE DOES'NT LEAVE OUT THE SOUL

3 John 1:2 (KJV) Beloved, I wish above all things that thou mayest prosper and be in health, even as thy soul prospereth.

SOME WOULD GLADLY GIVE UP WEALTH FOR HEALTH

DO YOU WANT YOUR BEST LIFE NOW?

remember that thou in thy lifetime receivedst thy good things, and likewise Lazarus evil things: but now he is comforted, and thou art tormented.

THERE ARE GUIDELINES IN THE WORD OF GOD
WHAT WAS IMPORTANT TO JESUS?
Matt 19: 22

Jesus said; if you want to be perfect sell what you have, and give to the poor

MAKE AN INVESTMENT

PASTOR RAYNER YOU SOUND LIKE A FOOL,
NO MORE THAN THE PASTOR WHO ASKS YOU FOR YOUR
RENT MONEY WITH NO SCRIPTURE TO BACK IT UP

21 Jesus said to him, "If you want to be perfect, go, sell what you have and give to the poor, and you will have treasure in heaven; and come, follow Me."

ONE GREAT HINDERANCE

FOR PROSPERITY TEACHERS

THERE IS SOMETHING GREATER THAN WEALTH

Can you put faith in wealth?

Prov 23:4-5

It appear**s in this day and age every preacher is trying to get rich.**

It appears as though the wisdom is earthly and causes them to love the world more than to love God. The Bible says that riches certainly make themselves wings; they fly away as an Eagle toward heaven.

RICHES ARE HERE TODAY, GONE TOMORROW

Riches are not eternal, they fly away

IT'S BETTER TO SEEK GODLY WISDOM

Riches are not eternal. Riches cannot be kept. Riches can take wings and fly away.

You are eternal. You were made by an eternal God, in his image. You were given eternal attributes, **such as Godly wisdom which is superior to man's wisdom.** In fact the Bible says the foolishness of God surpasses the wisdom of men!

PITY ON THE POOR, YOU LEND TO THE LORD

Prov 19:17
This is another way to invest into the kingdom of heaven. The word of God says to put your treasures in heaven. When the word of God says that

Jesus felt compassion and when about healing, even though healing was the action, compassion was the investment. Don't get me wrong, we need both to get your treasure to heaven, but if you have pity on the poor, and that word pity is an action word, because not only is their empathy, but there is also a giving in response to the pity. God says that he will pay again.

TREASURES IN HEAVEN

Matt 6:19 (KJV) *Lay not up for yourselves treasures upon earth, where moth and rust doth corrupt, and where thieves break through and steal*

Earthly treasures will last only in the earth. Heavenly treasures will take you from earth to heaven.

YOUR HEART WILL FOLLOW YOUR TREASURE

Matt 6:21
Do you want to stay in the earth? Don't get me wrong I know that we will rule the earth and after going to heaven we will return to the earth, for what I am saying is do you not want to go to heaven; to the wedding; to have the very highest status you can have with God. I believe that that's the reason for tithing. Putting your treasure where the real you desires to go. An act which requires you to apply your faith with works.

*RICHES REQUIRE YOU TO OBEY THEM. TO COVET in order to GET MORE

IF YOUR WILL IS TO BE RICH / YOU MAY FALL INTO SNARES

1 Tim 6:9-12 (KJV) But they **that will be rich** fall into temptation and a snare, and *into* many foolish and hurtful lusts, which drown men in destruction and perdition. **10** For the love of money is the root of all evil:

ONCE YOU RECIEVE WEALTH; IF YOUR HEART IS NOT RIGHT, THE DEVIL IS HALF WAY THERE IN IMPLEMENTING HIS PLAN

ERRING FROM THE FAITH

1 Tim 6:9-12

Many will tell you while preaching that it is God's good pleasure and prosper his servants. Although this is true we must examine prosper, because1 Tim 6:9-12 also says that they that desire to be rich fall into temptation and a snare, and into many foolish and hurtful lusts, which drown men in destruction and perdition. It goes on to say that the love of money is the root of all evil: which while some coveted after they have erred from the faith, and pierced themselves through with many sorrows. It then says to flee these things and follow righteousness. That tells me that while you are following covetousness you are not in righteousness, therefore the money loving preachers have erred from the faith and are no longer following God but they are following the money. These preachers may not even know it but they have stopped fighting the good fight of faith, to lay hold on to eternal life. That's where they were called to.

Perdition = Damnation / Eternal punishment in hell.

* WHY TALK ABOUT MONEY?

BECAUSE YOU MAY HAVE TO CHOOSE BETWEEN **YOUR** EARTHLY KINGDOM AND THE HEAVENLY KINGDOM

WHICH WILL YOUR HEART CHOOSE?

Matt 6:19-21 (KJV) Lay not up for yourselves treasures upon earth, where moth and rust doth corrupt, and where thieves break through and steal: 20 But lay up for yourselves treasures in heaven, where neither moth nor rust doth corrupt, and where thieves do not break through nor steal: **21 For where your treasure is, there will your heart be also.**

WHAT DO YOU CONSIDER TREASURE?

Lay not up for yourselves treasures upon earth, where moth and rust doth corrupt, and where thieves break through and steal:

I'D RATHER HAVE HEAVENLY TREASURES AND DESIRE TO BE WITH JESUS

ETERNITY IS A LONG TIME

BY THE TIME A SPARROW FLIES TO THE END OF THE UNIVERSE AND RETURNS ETERNITY WILL NOT YET HAVE BEGUN
AND THE UNIVERSE HAS NEVER STOPPED GROWING

DO YOU WANT YOUR BEST LIFE NOW?

OR ETERNITY?

WHERE IS YOUR HEART?

Luke 9:23-24 And he said to *them* all, If any *man* will come after me, let him deny himself, and take up his cross daily, and follow me. For whosoever will save his life shall lose it: but **whosoever will lose his life for my sake, the same shall save it.**

THE LOVE OF MONEY IS THE ROOT OF ALL EVIL

DO YOU HAVE IT OR DOES IT HAVE YOU?

1. YOU CAN HAVE IT, AND BLESS MANY, AND YOURSELF
2. IF IT HAS YOU, IT COMPELS YOU TO LUST FOR MORE

LOOKS LIKE GODLINESS

2 Tim 3:5 Having a **form of godliness,** but denying the power thereof**: from such turn away.**

TURN AWAY FROM THOSE WHO TEACH SUCH THINGS

This form of godliness denies the power the Holy Spirit, and therefore is a lukewarm gospel. This form of godliness does not attain to the things that happened in the book of acts. It does not believe in the power of God and therefore the Holy Spirit cannot be their comforter, he cannot be their mediator, advocate, stand by, teacher, and healer, miracle worker. The things that make a Christian stand out from religion. The word of God says **from such turn away.** Paul said I come not with craftiness of words, not with the form of godliness, but in the power of the Holy Ghost.

GAIN MAY LOOK LIKE GODLINESS, BUT IT'S NOT

* SOME TEACH THAT GAIN IS GODLINESS. THE BIBLE SAYS THEY HAVE CORRUPT MINDS, AND THEY ARE DESTITUE OF THE TRUTH.

HOW ARE YOU DOING?

I'M BLESSED AND HIGHLY FAVORED.

ARE YOU?   ARE YOU??

SATAN DON'T MIND GIVING A BILLION DOLLARS TO A PERSON WHO WILL SELL HIS SOUL TO HIM

YOUR SOUL IS WORTH OVER A TRILLION TIMES THAT

(EVEN PRICELESS), AND HE KNOWS IT

Satan wants your soul

WHEN HE GETS YOU TO PERFORM DISGUSTING AND INHUMANE ACTS OF DEBAUCHERY, YOU MAKE HIM FEEL LIKE A GOD. **AND HE LOVES IT!**

SATAN WILL OFFER YOU THE WORLD

1 Tim 6:5-6 Perverse disputings of men of corrupt minds, and destitute of the truth, **supposing that gain is godliness**: from such **withdraw thyself.**

THIS MEANS THAT YOU CAN BE BOUGHT **WITHDRAW YOURSELF** IF THE PERSON SUPPOSES GAIN IS GODLINESS.

SUPPOSE = TO ASSUME OR PRESUME WITHOUT ESTABLISHED PROOF.

THE DEVIL OFFERED JESUS THE WORLD
IT MAKES HIM FEEL LIKE HE'S GOD

Matt 4:8-10 (NKJV) Again, the devil took Him up on an exceedingly high mountain, and showed Him all the kingdoms of the world and their glory. 9 And he said to Him, "All these things I will give You if You will fall down and worship me." 10 Then Jesus said to him, "Away with you, Satan! For it is written, 'You shall worship the Lord your God, and Him only you shall serve.'

Jesus said to him, "Away with you, Satan! For it is written, 'You shall worship the Lord your God, and Him only you shall serve.'

YES; HE COULD HAVE GIVEN IT TO HIM, FOR A SEASON

WHEN THE FIRST MAN ADAM OBEYED SATAN: HE GAVE THE WORLD TO SATAN, BECAUSE SATAN THEN BECAME HIS MASTER.
NOW SATAN IS THE PRINCE OF THE POWER OF THE AIR
ADAM GAVE SATAN THIS WORLD

JESUS BOUGHT IT BACK, BECAUSE HE WOULD NOT COMPROMISE. **(YOUR ETERNAL LIFE WAS AT STAKE)** JESUS LOVED YOU ENOUGH TO NOT ONLY BUY YOU BACK FROM SATAN, BUT ALSO THE EARTH THAT HE HAD ORIGINALLY GIVEN TO US.

NOW SATAN IS SEEN AS THE PRINCE AND THE POWER OF THE AIR, BY THOSE WHO ARE HIS.
Eph 2:1-2 (KJV) Wherein in time past ye walked according to the course of this world, according to the prince of the power of the air, the spirit that now worketh in the children of disobedience:

JESUS LOVED YOU ENOUGH TO DO THIS FOR YOU

But godliness with contentment is great gain

GODLINESS IS SATISFYING

2 Tim 6:6.
Are you content? 2 Tim 6:6 says that godliness contentment is great gain. You can be in content and knowing that you will live all eternity in a place like heaven and with Christ. We brought nothing into the world and we can take nothing out of this world. One of the most authentic quotes ever is that I had never seen a hearse with a trailer behind

ABUNDANT LIFE

IS NOT JUST ABOUT MONEY

it doesn't leave out the soul

SOUL = INTELLECT, WILL, AND EMOTIONS
3 John 1:2 (Darby) Beloved, I desire that in all things thou shouldest prosper and be in health, even as thy soul prospers.

WHAT IF YOU WERE TOO SICK TO ENJOY RICHES
3 John 1:2 (NKJV) Beloved, I pray that you may prosper in all things and be in health, just as your soul prospers

ABUNDANT LIFE = A FULL SUPPLY
A FULL SUPPLY OF WHAT?
HEALTH, JOY, PEACE of MIND, LOVE, AND MONEY
These are some of the issues of life, that makes the abundant life.

DON'T COVET, AND CHASE WEALTH
THE SHEPHERD WANTS TO LEAD HIS SHEEP
John 10:10-11 (KJV) I am come that they might have life, and that they might have it more abundantly. 11 I am the good shepherd: the good shepherd giveth his life for the sheep.
But we learn to follow Christ he is the leader, he is the Shepherd. He lead us into green pastures. He lead us beside still waters. It is he that prepares us a place in the presence of our enemies.

SATAN HATES YOU; WHY?
BECAUSE YOU LOOK TOO MUCH LIKE GOD
SATAN WOULD LOVE TO SEE YOU MISERABLE, AND HE WILL GIVE YOU RICHES IN EXCHANGE FOR YOUR SOUL AND PUT ENOUGH DEPRESSION UPON YOU, AND AFTER YOU COMMIT SUICIDE; HE COLLECTS

MADE IN GODS IMAGE

Gen 1:26-28 (NKJV) <u>**So God created man in His own image;**</u> in the image of God He created him; male and female He created them. 28 Then God blessed them, and God said to them, "Be fruitful and multiply; fill the earth and subdue it; have dominion over the fish of the sea, over the birds of the air, and over every living thing that moves on the earth."

IT'S ALL ABOUT A WEDDING

The young man goes to the potential father-in-law, with 3 items to negotiate for his daughter's hand in marriage.

1. a large dowry, 2. a contract, 3. a skin of wine.
the young man and the girl's father discuss the terms.The cup is the seal or ratifier of the covenant.The young man pours some wine into a cup; if the father agrees with the young man, he calls for the daughter to comes forth.If the daughter agrees to marry this man, she drinks the wine, which **ratifies the betrothal of the marriage**. The covenant of betrothal is so strong it would take a writ of divorce to put her away, even though the marriage is not consummated.

THE POTENTIAL BRIDEGROOM OFFERED THE BRIDES FATHER 3 THINGS

These three things ratify the marriage. The dowry was given to our father in heaven. This was when Jesus gave his life for his bride. You were bought with a price, not with corruptible things such as silver and gold with the precious blood of Jesus. There was a contract that was given

A DOWERY / A gift or money brought by a man to her father for his bride.

The covenant was given as something that we need to keep. For the covenant both parties are obligated to do something. Jn 14:23 Jesus answered and said unto him, If a man love me, he will keep my word: and my Father will love him, and we will come unto him, and make our abode with him.

Jesus and the father will make their abode with him who loves him and keeps his word.

A CONTRACT / A covenant or written commitment enforceable by law.

Psm 116:13 I will take the cup of salvation, And call upon the name of Jehovah.

A CUP / The signing, authorizing, giving consent to, making officially valid. **The ratifying of the covenant**
THE DOWERY ACCEPTED, THE CONTRACT KEPT, THE CUP RATIFIED OR PUT ALL IN BINDING AGREEMENT.

THE DOWERY (JESUS'S LIFE)
Jn 10:18 No one taketh it away from me, but I lay it down of myself. I have power to lay it down, and I have power to take it again. This commandment received I from my Father

Jn 15:13 Greater love hath no man than this, that a man lay down his life for his friends. 14 Ye are my friends, if ye do the things which I command you.

Jn 3:16 For God so loved the world, that he gave his only begotten Son, that whosoever believeth on him should not perish, but have eternal life.

1Cor 6:20 for ye were bought with a price: glorify God therefore in your body.

1Cor 7:23 Ye were bought with a price; become not bondservants of men.

1 Pet 1:18 knowing that ye were redeemed, not with corruptible things, with silver or gold, from your vain manner of life handed down from your fathers; 19 but with precious blood, as of a lamb without spot, *even the blood* of Christ:

THE CONTRACT - THE WORD

OPPORTUNITY FOR OBEDIENCE

PSALM 138:2 I will worship toward thy holy temple, And give thanks unto thy name for thy lovingkindness and for thy truth: For thou hast magnified thy word above all thy name.

My Word above my name

We must keep the word of God. That is our agreement. It is a covenant. When two people have a covenant, they enter in with the intent of keeping their part.

People enter a covenant or contract for various reasons. Normally they each have a specific gift the other doesn't have. The greatest between a man and a woman is that the woman can give birth. Why would two women enter this covenant, or two men. Neither can have children without the other. The husband is the protector of the family; and the provider. The wife is the homemaker and the nurturer. Her role is to feed the children, nurture their development, and to be a support, and encourager, to both her husband and her children.

WE HAD NOTHING TO GIVE BUT OUR SIN
AND THE COVENANT WAS RATIFIED BY JESUS BLOOD

Jn 8:15 If ye love me, ye will keep my commandments. 16 And I will pray the Father, and he shall give you another Comforter, that he may be with you for ever, 17 *even* the Spirit of truth: whom the world cannot receive; for it beholdeth him not, neither knoweth him: ye know him; for he abideth with you, and shall be in you.

Jn 14:23 Jesus answered and said unto him, If a man love me, he will keep my word: and my Father will love him, and we will come unto him, and make our abode with him.

THE CUP

Wine was poured into the cup and if the bride consented; she drank *Psm 116:13 I will take the cup of salvation, And call upon the name of Jehovah.*

Luk22:42 Jesus was only about a stone cast away when he knelt down to pray, and said father if it be thou will remove this cup from me. Nevertheless not my will but father I'll do your will.

Mat 26:39 And he went forward a little, and fell on his face, and prayed, saying, My Father, if it be possible, let this cup pass away from me: nevertheless, not as I will, but as thou wilt.

*If the cup had been taken away Jesus would not be coming for the bride.

FATHER; TAKE AWAY THIS CUP

Luke 22:42 (NKJV) saying, "Father, if it is Your will, take this cup away from Me; **nevertheless not My will, but Yours, be done."**

THANK YOU JESUS; YOU DIDN'T HAVE
TO DIE FOR ME, BUT YOU DID.

You drank of the cup for me

MAY WE PRAY?

Are you going through relationship problems?
Are you depressed?
Do you need healing?
Are you unsure of your salvation?
Are you unsure if there's a heaven or hell?

**Let me pray with you a prayer that is guaranteed for God
to hear you.**

PLEASE PRAY THIS PRAYER FROM YOUR HEART

Dear heavenly father I come before you a sinner.
*I believe you sent your son to the earth to live for me, and to die for me,
and raised from the dead for me, so that I can experience eternal life, and
not hell. Thank you for bearing my sins, so that I don't have to. Come into
my heart, and live through me, so that I may live for you. Thank you Lord
for saving me.*

If you prayed this prayer in faith, please direct correspondence to:

HEAVENLY BOUND
James H. Rayner
PO Box #235
6425 LEORNARDTOWN RD
BRYANTOWN, MD. 20617

Reflection

WHERE

JEWISH CUSTOM

After the bridegroom negotiated with the father of the bride, and return home to his father, to begin building onto the father's house, once finished, he then returns for his bride at the command of the father.

When the bridegroom returns, he's going to return for one who is qualified to be his wife. Jesus's standard is for a **church without spot or wrinkle or blame or any such thing.** One who has kept their garments, and will not be before him in nakedness and shame.

All the church has to do is: keep your lamps full of oil and your wicks trimmed.

WHERE WILL YOU SPEND ETERNITY?

There are things that are important above all else. The first thing that is of utmost importance is that we __watch and pray always that we may be found worthy to escape the tribulation__, and that we may go up in the rapture. I cannot stress enough this importance. We have time to fill our lamps, we have time to prepare and to do the things of obedience that the Bible teaches, and that the Holy Ghost directs and leads us into. We have time to get rid of every spot and every blemish.

I'm saying to you; before, during, and, or after the rapture, which ever applies to you, "__Where will you spend eternity?__"

There is a question as to whether you will go in the rapture, but there is also a greater question, which is where will you spend eternity?

Are you confident?

2 Cor 5:8 Paul says here we are confident I say in willing rather to be absent from the body, and to be present with the Lord.
When that day comes and you are absent from your body you will be present with the Lord to be judged.
Wouldn't you like to go to heaven or are you one who do not care enough to miss hell?

God so loved me

PUT YOUR NAME HERE / **God so loved me:** *Jimmy*
John 3:16 (KJV) For God so loved *the world*, that he gave his only begotten Son, *that whosoever* believeth in him should not perish, but have everlasting life.
God so loved you that he gave his only begotten son so that you don't have to go to hell, but instead you can have everlasting life.

WATCH AND PRAY ALWAYS TO ESCAPE THE TRIBULATION

Luke 21:36. We must <u>watch and pray always that we may be counted worthy to escape</u> these things that shall come to pass, and I believe these things spoken of art things of the tribulation. We shall stand before the son of God.

The second thing of utmost importance is like that of the first; you do not want to be found as one who does not make the rapture. The word of God says blessed are those who go in the first resurrection for the second death has no power. You can still be a part of the first resurrection and stand before the Lord clean. We must understand that those of the second death have no power are not going to rise the same as in the rapture.

Those of the first resurrection shall reign with him
Rev 20:6 (KJV) Blessed and holy is he that hath part in the first resurrection: on such the second death hath no power, but they shall be priests of God and of Christ, and shall reign with him a thousand years.

Heb 9:27 (NKJV) And as it is appointed for men to die once, but after this the judgment,

WHERE WILL YOU SPEND ETERNITY?

I'm not saying that if you miss the rapture there is no hope left; I am however saying what the word of God says:

Heb 9:27 (NKJV) And as it is appointed for men to die once, but after this the judgment,

YOUR SOUL IS FOREVER

So whether you go in the rapture or after; you will spend eternity some where. WILL IT BE IN HEAVEN OR HELL. **YOUR SOUL IS FOREVER**

TWO PLACES - NO IN BETWEEN

*God has **prepared** two places*
*THE SAME WORD **PREPARE** IS USED*

PREPARE / In greek
HETOIMAZO / means; made ready or to make ready

I GO TO __PREPARE__ A PLACE FOR YOU

John 14:2-3 (NKJV) *In My Father's house are many mansions; if it were not so, I would have told you. I go to* **__prepare__** *a place for you. 3 And if I go and prepare a place for you, I will come again and receive you to Myself; that where I am, there you may be also.*

__PREPARED__ *FOR THE DEVIL AND HIS ANGELS*
Matt 25:41 (NKJV) *Then He will also say to those on the left hand, 'Depart from Me, you cursed, into the everlasting fire* **__prepared__** *for the devil and his angels*

YOU MUST CHOOSE; THE GLORY OF HEAVEN OR THE DISCRACE OF HELL

WHAT WE HAVE TO LOOK FORWARD TO:
NOT ONLY TO BE JOINED TO THE KING OF KINGS AND LORD OF LORDS BUT WE WILL BE CROWNED, AND REWARDED.

Let us start with what we need to apsire to heaven, what to run for, and what to attain to.
so ye would abound more and more. **2** For ye know what commandments we gave you by the Lord Jesus. **3 For this is the will of God, *even* your sanctification,** that ye should abstain from fornication:
* Because the Holy Spirit has come, he has given you the ability to abstain from fornication and that is Gods will.
SANCTIFICATION IS WHAT MAKES YOU DIFFERENT FROM THE WORLD

MAKE NO MISTAKE; YOU CANNOT TAKE YOUR SIN TO HEAVEN

As you abstain from fornication you stay sanctified which is to be separated from the world. You were sanctified when you received Christ as your Savior, but to remain sanctified is to abstain from fornication, less you have to repent as shown in 1 John 1: 9

TO BE CAUGHT UP WITH HIM

1 Thess 4:17 (KJV) This Scripture says that the dead in Christ shall rise first. When the word of God speaks of Jesus returning with his Saints; these Saints will come into the earth and pick up their bodies from the grave and return with those who remain, that shall be caught up. If Jesus can turn water into wine I'm quite sure he can turn a decomposed body into a glorious one. Then we which are alive *and* remain shall be caught up together with them in the clouds, to meet the Lord in the air: and **so shall we ever be with the Lord.**

JESUS wants us with him
He wants us caught up
He wants us raptured
Jesus wants us snatched out of the way of danger

Mal 3:5-6 (KJV) For I am the LORD, I change not; therefore ye sons of Jacob are not consumed.

SEE THE CHAPTER ON THE FEASTS OF ISRAEL AND THE RAPTURE
We must be as the barley and allow the Holy Spirit the wind, to blow away the chaff or the sin from your life.

THIS IS TRUE LIFE

THAT HE MAY CHANGE MY VILE BODY

To be like his

Phil 3:20-21

We look for the Savior the Lord Jesus Christ, for it is he who will turn these vile bodies to be fashioned like unto his glorious body and I base that on the fact that he is able to subdue all things unto himself for he is God.

REJOICE

We shall receive a glorified body. Jesus shall change our vile body to be like his. And we cannot yet comprehend this but we know it's good because we shall be like him, and if we love him we rejoice.

WE SHALL BE LIKE HIM

1 John 3:2-3 we do not know what we will be but we know that when Jesus appears we will be like him and we knows that everyone who has this hope purifies himself.

This hope of his coming purifies you and purifies you as he is pure. The word pure also means holy. Holiness is the unspotted over garment that will allow you to see God.

WHERE WILL YOU SPEND ETERNITY?

THE PURE IN HEART SHALL SEE GOD

Matt 5:7-8 (KJV) Blessed are the pure in heart: for they shall see God.

WITHOUT HOLINESS NO MAN SHALL SEE GOD

Heb 12:14 (KJV) Follow peace with all men, and holiness, without which no man shall see the Lord:

The pure in heart shall see God, and the holy shall see God so to be holy you must be pure in heart, and by being pure in heart you are made holy.

The worst thing you can do is allow a scoffer or blocker to turn you around. The Bible speaks of them for a reason.

They may be in your family. They may be your friends at work or at school, or even someone you just come across or meet. Normally as someone of a different religion, but I'm not giving you religion.

I'm giving you truth

WHERE IS YOUR HOPE? **IS THERE OPPOSITION?**

1. OPPOSITION FROM YOU; AND DO YOU HAVE THE FAITH TO DENY YOURSELF RATHER THAN JESUS.
Matt 16:24 Then said Jesus unto his disciples, If any *man* will come after me, let him deny himself, and take up his cross, and follow me.

2. OPPOSITION FROM SCOFFERS AND MOCKERS ALSO. THIS DOCTRINE IS THE BLESSED HOPE. THE WORLD HAS NO HOPE

2 Peter 3:3 Knowing this first, that there shall come in the last days scoffers, walking after their own lusts,

WE HAVE A HOPE

1 Cor 15:16-19 (KJV)
For if the dead rise not, then is not Christ raised: And if Christ be not raised, your faith *is* vain; ye are yet in your sins. Then they also which are fallen asleep in Christ are perished. **If in this life only we have hope in Christ, we are of all men most miserable.**

WHERE WILL YOU SPEND ETERNITY?

ARE YOU LISTENING TO

SCOFFERS AND MOCKERS

SCOFFERS DO NOT BELIEVE THE WORD OF GOD

JESUS IS HIS WORD. HE SAID HE'D RETURN. DO YOU BELIEVE IT.

*A scoffer says: "Where is the promise of His coming?

Scoffers Walk according to their own lusts,

DON'T LISTEN TO PRIDE

THEY SAY I KNOW WHEN; I KNOW WHEN HE'S COMING
2 Peter 3:3 (KJV) Knowing this first, that there shall come in the last days scoffers, **walking after their own lusts,**

Scoffers have not the spirit

IF THEY HAD THE SPIRIT, THEY WOULD HUMBLE THEMSELVES TO THE WORDS OF JESUS WHO PLAINLY TELLS US THESE THINGS ARE PUT IN THE AUTHORITY OF GOD (THE FATHER)

Jude 1:18-19 (KJV) How that they told you there should be mockers in the last time, who should walk after their own ungodly lusts. **19** These be they who separate themselves, sensual, **having not the Spirit.**

19 These be they who separate themselves,
THEY SEPERATE THEMSELVES FROM THOSE WHO SPEAK TRUE DOCTRINE

1. Scoffers Walk according to their own lusts,
2. Scoffers have not the spirit

HOPE

There are many Christians without a hope. They can't discern the Spirit, and they believe every spirit, but the Holy Spirit. The world is in the church, and teachers are doing everything but teaching.

Scoffers are those who are moved by their own lusts, and have not the Spirit

SCOFFERS WILL COME

2 Peter 3:2-4 (NKJV) that you may be mindful of the words which were spoken before by the holy prophets, and of the commandment of us, the apostles of the Lord and Savior, knowing this first: that scoffers will come in the last days, **walking according to their own lusts, and saying, "Where is the promise of His coming?** For since the fathers fell asleep, all things continue as they were from the beginning of creation."

THE QUESTION IS

Do not listen when scoffers question whether Jesus is to come, or tell you that he has delayed his coming.

Scoffers say:" where is the promise of Jesus coming? "He has delayed his coming. QUESTION: If he never told you when he'd return, and he don't know himself when he'll return; then how can you know if he is delayed?

DO YOU PLEASE THE MASTER?

THE TWO SERVANTS

*Matt 24:45-51 (KJV) Who then is a faithful and wise servant, whom his lord hath made ruler over his household, to give them meat in due season? Blessed is that servant, whom his lord when he cometh shall find so doing. Verily I say unto you, That he shall make him ruler over all his goods. **But and if that evil servant shall say in his heart, My lord delayeth his coming; And shall begin to smite his fellowservants, and to eat and drink with the drunken;** The lord of that servant shall come in a day when he looketh not for him, and in an hour that he is not aware of, And shall cut him asunder, and appoint him his portion with the hypocrites: there shall be weeping and gnashing of teeth.*

THE FAITHFUL AND WISE SERVANT / HE WILL BE BLESSED / HE SERVED THE MASTER AND WATCHED

Who then is a faithful and wise servant, whom his lord hath made ruler over his household, to give them meat in due season?

THE EVIL SERVANT (SCOFFER) DESIRE TO WALK AFTER HIS OWN LUST

But and if that evil servant shall say in his heart, My lord delayeth his coming; And shall begin to smite his fellowservants, and to eat and drink with the drunken.

MOCKERS, SCOFFERS, GRUMBLERS, AND COMPLAINERS

CAN'T HELP BUT ACT OUT (they don't have the Spirit.)

Jude 1:16-19 (NKJV) These are grumblers, complainers, walking according to their own lusts; and they mouth great swelling words, flattering people to gain advantage. 17 But you, beloved, remember the words which were spoken before by the apostles of our Lord Jesus

Christ: 18 how they told you that there would be mockers in the last time who would walk according to their own ungodly lusts. 19 **These are sensual persons, who cause divisions, not having the Spirit.**

Have you noticed they complain, make predictions, don't believe the word of God. They have their own way of thinking about what Jesus has said? They are not led by the Spirit who is the true teacher.

*THEIR SOUL PURPOSE IS TO CAUSE DIVISION
GRUMBLERS, COMPLAINERS, SCOFFERS, AND
MOCKERS

*Jude 1:16-19
People who are grumblers and complainers walk according to their own lust. When they speak great things it is to flatter people in order to gain advantage remember the words spoken before by the apostles of Jesus Christ who told you there would be mockers in the last day who would walk according to their own ungodly lusts. These are people who are sensual ruled by the flesh, and who causes division because they do not have the Spirit.
Flattering people to gain advantage.

THIS SHOWS THAT THEY ARE NOT EVEN
COMMITTED TO THEIR OWN WORDS

*Very agreeable when they can gain an advantage.
*Mockers walk according to their own ungodly lusts.
*These are sensual persons, who cause divisions, not having the Spirit.
*Scoffers and mockers, have not the Spirit, and they scoff just to cause division.

MARK THOSE WHO CAUSE DIVISION

*iF ONE TEACHES UNDER THE ADMONISION OF THE HOLY
GHOST AND ANOTHER TEACHES LED BY THEIR LUST*

THERE IS GOING TO BE DIVISION, AND THE SCOFFER IS THE CAUSE. MARK THEM.

CAN TWO WALK TOGETHER UNLESS THEY AGREE?

Rm 16:8 mark those who cause divisions, and offences contrary to the doctrine you have learned.

DON'T DISLOCATE SCRIPTURE, AND RUIN THE HEARER

2 Tim 2:14-21

We cannot afford to make mistakes or to misinterpret or to wrongly teach the word of God, because God's word is truth and it is his word that profits. We must be diligent to keep God's word in order that we may be approved by God. We must be a worker not ashamed, rightly dividing the word of truth. We cannot afford to hear profane and idle babblings for they increase more and more to ungodliness. And their message will spread like cancer. Hymenaeus and Philetus are of this sort, who have strayed concerning the truth, saying that the resurrection is already past; and they overthrow the faith of some. We must make sure we don't overthrow the faith of others. Give them hope. Nevertheless the solid foundation of God stands, having this seal. Who names the name of Christ, depart from iniquity." But in a great house there are not only vessels of gold and silver, but also of wood and clay, some for honor and some for dishonor. Therefore if anyone cleanses himself from the latter, he will be a vessel for honor, sanctified and useful for the Master, prepared for every good works.

MARK THOSE WHO SPEAK AGAINST JESUS RETURN

*Those who speak against the return of Jesus should be marked. They cause division.

Paul had a conflict with Hymenaeus and Philetus because of their profane and vain babblings.

<u>GUARD YOUR EARS</u>

<u>PAUL SAID THAT THEIR MESSAGE WOULD SPREAD LIKE A CANCER, SO MARK THEM</u>

*THEY WERE TELLING PEOPLE THAT THE RESURRECTION HAD ALREADY PASSED. **<u>THEY VIOLATE HOPE.</u>***

Faith comes by hearing, but so does fear.

Romans 10:17 (KJV)

So then faith *cometh* by hearing, and hearing by the word of God.

Where will you spend eternity?

Do you need prayer?

Are you going through relationship problems?
are you depressed?
Do you need healing?
Are you unsure of your salvation?
Are you unsure if there's a heaven or hell?
Let me pray with you a prayer that is guaranteed for God to hear you.

<u>PLEASE PRAY THIS PRAYER FROM YOUR HEART</u>

Dear heavenly father I come before you a sinner.
I believe you sent your son to the earth to live for me, and to die for me, and raised from the dead for me, so that I can experience eternal life, and not hell. Thank you for bearing my sins, so that I don't have to. Come into

my heart, and live through me, so that I may live for you. Thank you Lord for saving me.

If you prayed this prayer in faith, please direct correspondence to:

HEAVEN BOUND
James H. Rayner
PO Box #235
6425 LEORNARDTOWN RD
BRYANTOWN, MD. 20617

Reflection

WHEN

Is The Rapture?

JEWISH CUSTOM

*The rapture cannot take place without the approval of the father, for it is in the authority of the father. When a Jewish wedding was to take place and while the potential bride was in the the betrothal stage of the marriage the bridegroom was to go and prepare a place for the bride. The father determines when it is time for the son to go get his bride and bring her home. That is when he goes to the son and says; **go get your bride.***

WE ARE CHILDREN OF THE LIGHT

1 Thess 5:4-7 (KJV) But ye, brethren, are not in darkness, that that day should overtake you as a thief. 5 Ye are all the children of light, and the children of the day: we are not of the night, nor of darkness. *Because we are children of the light, that day will not overtake us. Even though we do not know when the rapture is to take place, we are the children of light, and we walk in the light. To be in the light means we do not do the things of darkness therefore Jesus comes as a thief in the night, we are not caught unaware because we have the light, and can see.*

WE ARE SOBER AND NOT ASLEEP

Therefore let us not sleep, as do others; but let us watch and be sober. For they that sleep sleep in the night; and they that be drunken are drunken in the night.

When is the rapture going to take place?
Pre-tribulation, mid-tribulation, or post-tribulation.

When is the rapture going to take place?
It is not for you to know the times or the seasons, which the Father hath
put in his own power. And because I'm a child of the late, and not a child
of the dark, I walk in the light and they're not undermine the authority of
the father.

We have thousands of ministers trying to tell us when.
What does God say about in his word?
It's time we begin to say what God has placed in his word.

Acts 1:6-7 (KJV) And he said unto them, It is not for you to know the times
or the seasons, which the Father hath put in his own power.

It is not for you to know the times or the seasons, which the Father hath
put in his own power, but you can read the word of God, and discern
based on what you see.

ARE YOU A FAITHFUL SERVANT?

Matt 24:46-47 (KJV) Blessed *is* that servant, whom his lord when
he cometh shall find so doing. **47** Verily I say unto you, That he shall
make him ruler over all his goods.

<u>Ultimately the rapture is when God says it is.</u>
God the father is showing his role as the father of the bridegroom.

His plan is for his son to come to the earth and get his bride for the
marriage supper of the Lamb, while the wrath of God, (tribulation),
is taking place on the earth. The word of God says that God has not
designed us for wrath. This means that the tribulation is not for us, but
if we neglect this great salvation, how shall we escape the tribulation.

I Heb 2:2-3 (KJV) How shall we escape, if we neglect so great salvation;

To be saved you must tend to your salvation. I'm not talking about being saved from sin and death. I'm talking about the things that are to come upon this earth. The things that the Bible speak of for the last days. The salvation I am speaking of is the one that is to snatch you out of the way of danger, (the tribulation).

PREPARE FOR THE WEDDING OF THE LAMB

WE MUST GET TO KNOW THE LORD

Matt 7:21-23

Can you imagine how many people will say: Lord Lord let me into the kingdom. And many of these have not done the will of the father. They will say did I not prophesy in your name?, Did not I cast out demons in your name?, Did I not do many wonderful works in your name?, And then the Lord will say to them I never knew you: depart from me, ye workers of iniquity.

Just to give an analogy of what I'm about to say; you cannot lose your first love if you never loved. Look at the consequences of the actions of the church who lost its first love.

*Nevertheless I have somewhat against thee, **because thou hast left thy first love.** 5 Remember therefore from whence thou art fallen, and repent, and do the first works; or else I will come unto thee quickly, and will remove thy candlestick out of his place, except thou repent.*

Rev 2:4-5 the Lord said: you have fallen, and tells the church to repent or he will come quickly and remove their candlestick. To me this means they will no longer be zealous of the Lord, but will be lukewarm with consequences.

*Can you see that everyone's not going to make it. Everyone is not going to go in to heaven just because they say Lord did'nt I do your works.
Mark 13:31-32

Not only do we not know the day or the hour, except the Father, but even the angels in heaven do not know when the rapture is to take place. Can you imagine Jesus don't know, the Angels don't know, and you don't know but only the Father knows.

WHEN WILL THE RAPTURE TAKE PLACE?

The closest I can say is; the rapture will take place after the antichrist is revealed and after the great falling away of the church.

2 Thess 2:3-4
There will be a falling away first, and then the man of sin shall be revealed. He is the son of perdition. He opposes God on every hand and he opposes all that is worshiped so that he sees himself as God.

YOU ARE NOT TO KNOW THE TIME OR SEASON

which the Father hath put in his own power.
Acts 1:6-7 (KJV) When they therefore were come together, they asked of him, saying, Lord, wilt thou at this time restore again the kingdom to Israel? And he said unto them, It is not for you to know the times or the seasons, which the Father hath put in his own power.

POWER = *EXOUSIA*
EXOUSIA = *Means Authority*
If your father says; we are going on vacation tomorrow, don't steal the car and go today. All is in the authority of your father.
It is God the Father's operation. It is his plan that will determine when JESUS WILL RETURN.

IT IS IN GOD'S AUTHORITY ONLY

We as men do not know the day or the hour of the second coming of Christ to the earth. All that we know is the times and seasons, which proves the nearness of the second coming.

WE CAN HOWEVER SEE WHEN THE RAPTURE IS CLOSE, BECAUSE OF THE EVENTS THE BIBLE GIVES, AND IN THE ORDER THEY ARE TO HAPPEN.

How dare we attempt to undermine the authority of God concerning something that only he knows.

YOU KNOW NOT THE TIMES AND SEASONS
1 Thess 5:1-2 **_But of the times and the seasons, brethren, ye have no need that I write unto you._** *2 For yourselves know perfectly that the day of the Lord so cometh as a thief in the night.*

BUT YOU ARE NOT IN DARKNESS
1 Thess 5:4-5 (KJV)
But ye, brethren, are not in darkness, that that day should overtake you as a thief. *5 Ye are all the children of light, and the children of the day: we are not of the night, nor of darkness.*

*We are not in darkness that the day should overtake us as a thief, being the children of light, we must walk in the light.

Christ did do a comparison of the days of Noah and the days just before his coming. He stated that men before the flood knew not until the flood came and took them all away. So also shall the coming of the Son of Man be.

There will be great regrets, from people who did not believe the rapture was coming. There are to be many people, who change their minds about God, and the church, and what they should be doing with their lives. There are going to be many who attempt to save their lives and will lose it, but those who lose their lives for the sake of Christ will surely find it.

GOD CLOSED THE DOOR AND IT BEGAN TO RAIN

Matt 24:37-39 *But as the days of Noe were, so shall also the coming of the Son of man be. For as in the days that were before the flood they were eating and drinking, marrying and giving in marriage, until the day that Noe entered into the ark, And knew not until the flood came, and took them all away; so shall also the coming of the Son of man be.*

THE WORLD WILL NOT BE AWARE OF WHAT'S COMING

THE LORD IS COMING
Jude 1:14 *And Enoch also, the seventh from Adam, prophesied of these, saying, Behold, the Lord cometh with ten thousands of his saints,*

DON'T SET DATES
WHY WOULD YOU AS A CHRISTIAN TRY TO USURP GODS AUTHORITY? GOD KNOWS, AND ONLY HE KNOWS

Certain religious cults spend much time in setting definite dates for the second coming of Jesus Christ, as well as for the rapture of the church and other events of prophecy. These dates are all based upon the fallacy that a day in prophecy means a year and the year means a day. certain statements of so many days in Scripture are interpreted to mean that same number of years. This has led some to predict the second Advent at different dates that are now in the past. You must understand that this day and hour was placed in the hands of the father. It is in his authority. Any prediction would be a violation and override of his authority.

THE BETROTHED

We who have received him as Savior are presently betrothed to Jesus Christ

Betrothal involved the establishment of a marriage covenant. The bridegroom would travel from his father's house to the home of the future bride. There he would negotiate with the father of the young woman to decide the price (mohar) that he must pay to purchase his bride. Once the bridegroom paid the purchase price, the marriage covenant was thereby established, and the young man and woman were regarded to be as husband and wife. From that moment on the bride was declared to be consecrated or sanctified, set apart exclusively for her bridegroom. (*This is where we; the church are presently, in Christ*). As a symbol of the covenant relationship that had been established, the groom would pour a cup of wine. If the bride drank from a cup of wine, over which a betrothal benediction had been pronounced, the betrothal was ratified and they then looked forward to the wedding ceremony, and the consummation of the marriage.

After the marriage covenant had been established, the groom would leave the home of the bride and return to his father's house. There he would remain separate from his bride for a period of at least twelve months. This period of separation afforded the bride time to gather her trousseau and to prepare for married life. The groom occupied himself with the preparation of living accommodations in his father's house to which he could bring his bride.

How dare the scoffer teacher disregard the father's authority to determine when the rapture should take place. Anything other than a preparation of his return and feeding the sheep, teaching them to hope for his return is unacceptable.

THE FATHER DECIDES WHEN

The time for his return, was totally in the hands of the father. After the portion of the house was built for the bridegroom and bride, the father determined when to say:

Go Get Your Bride

Meanwhile the bride to be; as per custom keeps a lamp filled with oil by her bed. Normally the call that the bridegroom is coming takes place at night. The bride awaits the call:

FOR US:

The **lamp** is the word of God
The **oil** is the Holy Spirit
The **wick was also trimmed** (the adorning of ones self)

Psalms 119:105 (KJV)
Thy word *is* a lamp unto my feet, and a light unto my path.

Matt 25:7 (KJV) Then all those virgins arose, and trimmed their lamps.

WHEN: SHE HEARS, "**THE BRIDE GROOM COMETH**" IT IS AT THAT TIME THAT SHE RISES AND PROCEEDS TO HER NEW LIFE.

BEHOLD THE BRIDEGROOM COMETH

Matt 25:5-8 (NKJV) But while the bridegroom was delayed, they all slumbered and slept. And at midnight a cry was heard: '**Behold, the bridegroom is coming;** go out to meet him!' Then all those virgins arose and trimmed their lamps. And the foolish said to the wise, 'Give us some of your oil, for our lamps are going out.'

IS YOUR LAMP FILLED?

Eph 5:18 (NKJV) And do not be drunk with wine, in which is dissipation; but **be filled with the Spirit.**

We are not to be worldly and drunk with wine, but our alternative is to be filled with the spirit of God.

IS YOUR LAMP FILLED? ARE YOU WATCHING?
ARE YOU PRAYING ALWAYS?

Luke 21:36 (NKJV) <u>Watch therefore, and pray always</u> that you may be counted worthy to escape all these things that will come to pass, and to stand before the Son of Man."

JOHN THE BAPTIST IS THE BEST MAN

At the end of the period of separation, the groom would come to take his bride to live with him. The taking of the bride usually took place at night. **The groom, best man** and other male escorts would leave the groom's father's house and conduct a torch light procession to the home of the bride. Although the bride was expecting her groom to come for her, she did not know the exact time of his coming. As a result the groom's arrival would be preceded by a shout. This shout would forewarn the bride to be prepared for the coming of the groom.

BEST MAN

BEST MAN - **Luke 7:28** For I say to you, among those **born of women there is not a greater prophet than John the Baptist;** but he who is least in the kingdom of God is greater than he."

The job of the best man is to help the bride groom get dressed.

The Holy Spirit is here to help us as the church to be adorned for the wedding. The Holy Spirit must help us to put on the things of God, and to take off the things of the world. We are also to be presentable and without spot or wrinkle or blame.

TO BE DRESSED

Matt 3:14-15 (NKJV) And John tried to prevent Him, saying, "I need to be baptized by You, and are You coming to me?" 15 But Jesus answered and said to him, "Permit it to be so now, **for thus it is fitting for us to fulfill all righteousness."** Then he allowed Him.

JOHN, NOT WORTHY, BUT

John was right. He was not worthy to help the master get dressed in his righteousness for the wedding.(This righteousness was performed at the Jordan when Jesus was baptized by John the Baptist). This is symbolic of the righteousness that he put on. But there is none greater born of a woman. John had to be filled with the Holy Ghost from his mother's womb, and live in the wilderness ; sanctified and uncontaminated by "so- called" civilization. (the world).

After the wedding, the best man stands at the door of the chamber (huppah), for the consummation of the marriage under the wedding that is taking place under the chuppah.

The bridegroom has the bride, and the friend or best man stands at the door and rejoices

John 3:29 (NKJV) He who has the bride is the bridegroom; but the friend of the bridegroom, who stands and hears him, rejoices greatly because of the bridegroom's voice. Therefore this joy of mine is fulfilled.

THE HOLY SPIRIT MUST GET THE BRIDE READY

After the groom received his bride together with her female attendants, the enlarged wedding party would return from the bride's home to the groom's father's house. Upon arrival there the wedding party would find that the wedding guests had assembled already. There will be a seven-day party.

Are you allowing the Holy Spirit to get you dressed?
The Holy Spirit will not only get you dressed, but will also take you to the wedding.

2 Thess 2:7-8 (NKJV) For the mystery of lawlessness is already at work; **only He who now restrains will do so until He is taken out of the way.** 8 And then the lawless one will be revealed, whom the Lord will consume with the breath of His mouth and destroy with the brightness of His coming

*He who now restrains will do so until He is taken out of the way.

THE HOLY GHOST NOW RESTRAINS
AFTER THE ONE WHO RESTRAINS SIN IS TAKEN OUT OF THE WAY; THEN THE MAN OF SIN WILL BE REVEALED. RIGHT NOW THE HOLY SPIRIT IS HOLDING HIM BACK.

YOU MUST BE DRESSED
TO GET MARRIED

Matt 22:11-14 (NKJV) But when the king came in to see the guests, he saw a man there who did not have on a wedding garment. So he said to him, 'Friend, how did you come in here without a wedding garment?' And he was speechless. Then the king said to the servants, 'Bind him hand and foot, take him away, and cast him into outer darkness; there will be weeping and gnashing of teeth.'

For many are called, but few are chosen."
MANY ARE CALLED AND HAVE TIME TO GET DRESSED, BUT IF YOU DON'T YOU DON'T ATTEND.

THERE ARE TWO GARMENTS
CHITON = *The undergarment. It clothes you.*
STOLE = *Very descriptive outerwear, such as for a king, a priest, a ruler, royalty. No one has to describe you. The glory is seen in your outer wear.*

CLOTHED IN CHITON AND STOLE
SALVATION AND RIGHTEOUSNESS

Isaiah 61:10 (NKJV) I will greatly rejoice in the Lord,
My soul shall be joyful in my God;

CLOTHED IN A GARMENT AND ROBED IN
RIGHTEOUISNESS

For He has clothed me with the garments of salvation,
He has covered me with the robe of righteousness,

THE STOLE AND JEWELS SHOW WHO YOU ARE
ROYALTY

As a bridegroom decks himself with ornaments,
And as a bride adorns herself with her jewels.

*JESUS PURCHASED OUR OUTER WEAR AS WELL AS THE
UNDERGARMENT. ALL YOU HAVE TO DO IS PUT IT ON,
WITH THE HELP OF THE HOLY SPIRIT*

Jesus purchased our salvation, as well as our righteousness.
JESUS IS SALVATION
Acts 4:12 (NKJV) *Nor is there salvation in any other, for there is no other name under heaven given among men by which we must be saved.*

THIS OUTER GARMENT TOLD WHO JESUS IS
BUT HE HAD TO BE CLOTHED WITH THE OUT GARMENT
Phil 2:5-8 (NKJV) *Let this mind be in you which was also in Christ Jesus who, being in the form of God, did not consider it robbery to be equal with God, but made Himself of no reputation, taking the form of a bondservant,*

and coming in the likeness of men. And being found in appearance as a man, He humbled Himself and became obedient to the point of death, even the death of the cross

He laid his glory down to be married to you
Phil 2:5-8 Show us where Jesus laid his glory down; as God. When he came into the earth born as a man it was because he had laid his glory down for this cause. He then picked up his being son of man, so a mere man or woman could pick up the glory he purchased for you, as the bride. Don't worry the Holy Spirit was sent to help you get dressed.

LET THIS MIND BE IN US

Phil 2:5-9 (KJV)
*We are told to let this mind be in us that was also in Christ Jesus. The mind that tells us; he thought it was okay to be **equal with God**, (thought it not robbery). The word of God says that he made himself of no reputation, and took upon himself the formal a servant, and was made in the likeness of men and being in the fashion of a man, he humbled himself and became obedient even unto death, the death of the cross. And because of all of this God highly exalted him, and gave him a name that is above every name. **ISOS** = EQUAL /likeness, the same in nature and dignity*

THIS HOUR IS FOR GLORY

John 12:27-28
Jesus was troubled, because he was about to go to the cross. It was his hour, it was his time. He asked the father to save him from this hour, and from this time. After his recant, he reflected, and came to the conclusion that this is the reason he came into the world. Then he said, father glorify thy name. The father said I have both glorified it, and will glorify it again.

HIS WIFE HAS MADE HERSELF READY

Rev 19:7-8

this passage of Scripture says will let us be glad and rejoice and give the Lord glory, for this is the time for the marriage of the Lamb. The marriage of the Lamb has come, and the one that was his bride has now become his wife, because she has done what was required of her, and have qualified resulting in making herself ready and because of this she has been granted to be arrayed in fine linen, clean and bright for the fine linen is the righteous acts of the Saints and is shown in the deck core of the city honoring her.

HE HAS CLOTHED ME WITH SALVATION AND RIGHTEOUSNESS

Isaiah 61:10 I will greatly rejoice in the Lord,
My soul shall be joyful in my God;
For He has clothed me with **the garments of salvation,**
He has covered me with **the robe of righteousness,**
As a bridegroom decks himself with ornaments,
And as a bride adorns herself with her jewels.

THE FILTHY GARMENT MUST BE REMOVED

Zech 3:3-4 (NKJV) Now Joshua was clothed with filthy garments, and was standing before the Angel. Then He answered and spoke to those who stood before Him, saying, "Take away the filthy garments from him." And to him He said, "See, I have removed your iniquity from you, and I will clothe you with rich robes.

We will be clothed in rich robes. People will know our purpose and who we are by what we wear.

BEFORE JESUS SAVED ME

Isaiah 64:6 (KJV)
But we are all as an unclean *thing*, and all our righteousnesses *are* as filthy rags; and we all do fade as a leaf; and our iniquities, like the wind, have taken us away.

A FEW HAVE SUSTAINED FROM FORNICATION

*Rev 3:4 (NKJV) You have a few names even in Sardis who have not defiled their garments; **and they shall walk with Me in white, for they are worthy.** When you walk with him in white, that is speaking of the wedding garment which is the righteousness of the Saints. The whole city will be done up in white, and linen speaking of the cleanness and sanctification of the Saints.*

YOU KEPT MY COMMAND; I WILL KEEP YOU

Rev 3:10
You will be From the trial that is coming upon the whole earth. The tribulation. Truly this church although it has little strength the Lord had no rebukes. He expressed his love and promise of protection from the trial coming upon the earth because this church His word with patience.

FLESH DEFILES THE GARMENT

Jude 1:23 but others save with fear, pulling them out of the fire, <u>hating even the garment defiled by the flesh.</u>

*Not that you have flesh, but that you walk in flesh. I believe, walking in the flesh is what defiles the garment. The word of God says that if you walk in the spirit you will not fulfill the lust flesh. Therefore there will be no way that you can defile your garment.

CONSUMMATION

Shortly after arrival the bride and groom would be escorted by the other members of the wedding party to the bridal chamber (huppah). Prior to entering the chamber the bride remained veiled so that no one could see her face. While the groomsmen and bridesmaids would wait outside, the bride and groom would enter the bridal chamber alone. There in the privacy of that place they would enter into physical union under the chuppah for the first time, thereby consummating the marriage that had been covenanted earlier.

bridal chamber (huppah).
bed canopy (chuppah)

WHEN IS THE RAPTURE?

Just as in previous teachings we were attempting to pinpoint a rational view on how close the rapture is, not overriding the authority of the father which we believe would be sin; so now we make no claims that we are right. We just want to add some clarity to the question of when.

AS IT WAS IN THE DAYS OF NOAH

Luke 17:26-37 (NKJV) 26 <u>And as it was in the days of Noah, so it will be also in the days of the Son of Man</u>: 27 They ate, they drank, they married wives, they were given in marriage, until the day that

NOAH ENTERED THE ARK, AND THEN THE FLOOD CAME

Noah entered the ark, and the flood came and destroyed all, but Noah and his family.
I believe we will be raptured and true tribulation will come. This is just the beginning.

The rapture - our ark of salvation

The tribulation - to be compared to Noah's flood.

Notice the flood came after Noah and his family were saved by the Ark that Noah had built. I've heard it called the Ark of salvation. I believe that the rapture is our Ark of salvation, that will take us out of the way of the tribulation.

AS IT WAS IN THE DAYS OF LOT

Likewise as it was also in the days of Lot: They ate, they drank, they bought, they sold, they planted, they built;

IN THE DAY LOT WENT OUT OF SODOM, IT RAINED FIRE AND BRIMSTONE.

The word of God says that in the day lot went out of Sodom it rained fire and brimstone. So when Lot and his family left the city that's when fire and brimstone hit the city.

AS THEY LEFT SODOM - it rained fire and brimstone
AS WE LEAVE EARTH - the tribulation will take place

SO SHALL IT BE WHEN THE SON OF MAN IS REVEALED
Even so will it be in the day when the Son of Man is revealed.

NOTICE GOD DELIVERS THOSE WHO ARE HIS

DO YOU TRUST JESUS?
2 Peter 2:9 (NKJV) the Lord knows how to deliver the godly out of temptations and to reserve the unjust under punishment for the day of judgment,

The Lord knows how to deliver the godly

JESUS IS INTERCEEDING FOR YOU
Heb 7:25 (NKJV) Therefore He is also able to save to the uttermost those who come to God through Him, since He always lives to make intercession for the saints.

DO YOU BELEIVE HE'LL SAVE YOU?
Psalms 55:16 (NKJV) As for me, I will call upon God, And the Lord shall save me.

GOD APPOINTED US TO OBTAIN SALVATION NOT WRATH

1 Thess 5:5-11 (NKJV) Therefore let us not sleep, as others do, but let us watch and be sober. For those who sleep, sleep at night, and those who get drunk are drunk at night. But let us who are of the day be sober, putting on the breastplate of faith and love, and as a helmet the hope of salvation. **For God did not appoint us to wrath, but to obtain salvation through our Lord Jesus Christ,** who died for us, that whether we wake or sleep, we should live together with Him. Therefore comfort each other and edify one another, just as you also are doing.

WE OBTAIN SALVATION HOW?
Whether we wake or sleep, we should live together with Him.
We obtain salvation through our Lord Jesus Christ,

OBTAIN = Hearing, calling, primary motion as in growing into. Implys you must continue in order to lay hold on to your salvation, motioning into maturity.

Rev 16:14-15 (KJV)
Behold, I come as a thief. Blessed *is* he that watcheth, and **keepeth his garments**, lest he walk naked, and they see his shame.

KEEP YOUR GARMENT CLEAN

TO OBTAIN WORTHINESS TO ESCAPE DAMNATION, IS TO OBTAIN SALVATION

Luke 21:35-36 (KJV) Watch ye therefore, and pray always, **that ye may be accounted worthy to escape all these things that shall come to pass,** and to stand before the Son of man.

HOW SHALL WE ESCAPE IF WE NEGLECT THIS SALVATION?

Heb 2:3-8 how shall we escape if we neglect so great a salvation, which at the first began to be spoken by the *Lord, and was confirmed to us by those who heard Him. God also bearing witness both with signs and wonders, with various miracles, and gifts of the Holy Spirit, according to His own will?*

For He has not put the world to come, of which we speak, in subjection to angels. 6 But one testified in a certain place, saying:

God made this way of escape for us that we should prepare and tend to our salvation. God bear witness with signs and wonders and various miracles and gifts of the Holy Spirit according to his own will, for he has not put the world to come in subjection to Angels. He said one testified in a certain place saying:

"What is man that You are mindful of him,
Or the son of man that You take care of him?
You have made him a little lower than the angels;
You have crowned him with glory and honor,
And set him over the works of Your hands.
You have put all things in subjection under his feet."

For in that He put all in subjection under him, He left nothing that is not put under him. But now we do not yet see all things put under him. But we see Jesus, who was made a little lower than the angels, for the suffering of death crowned with glory and honor, that He, by the grace of God, might taste death for everyone.

DO YOU NEED PRAYER?

Are you going through relationship problems?
Are you depressed?
Do you need healing?
Are you unsure of your salvation?
Are you unsure if there's a heaven or hell?
Let me pray with you a prayer that is guaranteed for God to hear you.

PLEASE PRAY THIS PRAYER FROM YOUR HEART
Dear heavenly father I come before you a sinner.
I believe you sent your son to the earth to live for me, and to die for me, and raised from the dead for me, so that I can experience eternal life, and not hell. Thank you for bearing my sins, so that I don't have to. Come into my heart, and live through me, so that I may live for you. Thank you Lord for saving me.

If you prayed this prayer in faith, please direct correspondence to:

HEAVEN BOUND
James H. Rayner
PO Box #235
6425 LEORNARDTOWN RD
BRYANTOWN, MD. 20617

Reflection

WHY

THE RAPTURE?

Anyone who has spent a great deal of time in God's presence, know that God does not do anything without a reason. Many times we miss the reason, and that is where we get religion, which many times becomes tradition.

JEWISH CUSTOM

We must understand that God's customs and traditions that he gave to the Jewish people, are precepts that will lead you to eternal life, and abundance. We are royalty, and a part of the son of God and a partaker of his inheritance.

THE GREATEST REASON; WHY THE RAPTURE? SUMMED UP IN SO MANY WORDS IS: TO BE WITH JESUS

John 14:2-3 (KJV)

In my Father's house are many mansions: if *it were* not *so*, I would have told you. I go to prepare a place for you. And if I go and prepare a place for you, I will come again, and receive you unto myself; **that where I am, *there* ye may be also.**

You hold the tradition of men

Mark 7:8-9
Lay aside tradition in ritualism. We have too many religions that tried to mystify and doing common things such as washing pots and

cups and occupying the minds of people bent towards tradition in ritualism and not towards the true word of God. These things cost people to not think about and or to reject the word of God. Jesus said why do you keep tradition yet not my word. He also said: your tradition has made my word of no effect. Receive the commandment of God even if you have the reject the tradition of men.

You made my word of no effect.

Mark 7:13 (KJV) Making the word of God of none effect through your tradition, which ye have delivered: and many such like things do ye.

JUST POLISHING THE MACHINERY

You may polish your car day and night; and even pop the hood and polished the engine, and it may be spotless inside and out, but if there's no oil in it, and no gas and it, you aren't going anywhere.

Polishing the machinery

Many church folk are polishing the machinery. Their religion looks good on the outside, because They do what they've seen their mothers do, and they do what they've seen the pastor do, and if they don't have the Holy Spirit which is equal to the oil, or the word of God in them which is equal to the gas, then they aren't going anywhere.

Full well ye reject the commandment of God, that ye may keep your own tradition.

Religion is man's search for God, Having a relationship with God, is when you have found God. If you have found God and are familiar with the tribulation that is about to come upon the whole earth, then you already know why the rapture is to take place.

God has not designed his people for wrath.

2 Peter 2:9 (KJV)
The Lord knoweth how to deliver the godly out of temptations, and to reserve the unjust unto the day of judgment to be punished:

WHY THE RAPTURE?

TO RECEIVE THE HARVEST
See the passages on God's harvest

1 Cor 15:21-23

Death came forth by man but by man also came the resurrection of the dead because in Adam all died, because of his transgression but in Christ, all were made alive because of what Jesus did, so all things shall be restored in their proper order; Christ the firstfruits and then those who are his at his coming.

IN CHRIST ALL SHALL BE MADE ALIVE (QUICKENED).

WE SHALL NOT ALL GO TO THE GRAVE
1 Cor 15:51-52 (KJV) _Behold, I shew you a mystery;_ **We shall not all sleep,** _but we shall all be changed, In a moment, in the twinkling of an eye, at the last trump: for the trumpet shall sound, and the dead shall be raised incorruptible, and we shall be changed._

WHY THE RAPTURE?

There are reasons why the rapture is to take place.

1. To get the overcoming church home.
If you noticed in the book of Revelation the faults of the church are mentioned and then the rewards for overcoming the faults. Each church is spoken of as the church, but the rewards are only for those who have overcome the

faults. If you look just a little deeper you will see that all of the rewards take place in heaven.

Notice: There are only three groups of people that this Bible speaks of an normally one at a time: they are the Jew, Gentile, and the church.

Immediately after the attention on the church ceases the very next chapter Revelations 4:1 <u>begins with come up here.</u> It appears as though the church is raptured at this point.

At this point there is no more mention of the church except those who are to die in the tribulation.

WHY THE RAPTURE?

2. TO PREPARE THE CHURCH FOR HEAVEN

The title says to prepare the church for heaven. We are prepared for heaven when we are changed. This passage of Scripture says that we shall not all sleep meaning that we shall not all die for going to heaven, but we shall be changed in a moment, in the twinkling of an eye, at the last Trump: for the trumpet shall sound and the dead shall be raised incorruptible and we shall be changed I want you to know that this change is necessary to prepare the church for heaven it says in an instant in a twinkling of twinkling is 1/100 of a second and the changes going to be from mortal to immortality, from corruptible incorruptible, because the first time Jesus came to change our spirits, to make us a new creature, but the second time he has come to change our bodies so that the whole man can go to heaven.

HEAVEN BOUND

THE FIRST COMING WAS FOR JESUS TO PREPARE YOUR SPIRIT

THE SECOND TIME HE COMES TO PREPARES THE BODY

WHY THE RAPTURE?

3. To reveal the antichrist

1 John 2:22 This Scripture says that it's a liar who denies that Jesus is the Christ and it is Antichrist at the ninth the father and the son.

WHY THE RAPTURE?

4. That we shall be with Christ for ever.

1 Thess 4:17 *Then we which are alive and remain shall be caught up together with them in the clouds, to meet the Lord in the air: and so shall we ever be with the Lord.*

WHY THE RAPTURE?

THAT GOD MAY BE GLORIFIED

We shall not all sleep

A mystery about the harvest

1 Cor 15:51-53 (KJV) Behold, I shew you a mystery; **We shall not all sleep,** but we shall all be changed, 52 In a moment, in the twinkling of an eye, at the last trump:

we shall be raised and therefore harvested

for the trumpet shall sound, and the dead shall be raised incorruptible, and we shall be changed. 53 **For this corruptible must put on incorruption, and this mortal must put on immortality.**

WHY THE RAPTURE?

TO SEPERATE the wheat and tares

Let the wheat and tares grow together

Matt 13:24-30 (NKJV) Another parable He put forth to them, saying: "The kingdom of heaven is like a man who sowed good seed in his field; but while men slept, his enemy came and sowed tares among the wheat and went his way. But when the grain had sprouted and produced a crop, then the tares also appeared. So the servants of the owner came and said to him, 'Sir, did you not sow good seed in your field? How then does it have tares?' He said to them, 'An enemy has done this.' The servants said to him, 'Do you want us then to go and gather them up?' But he said, **'No, lest while you gather up the tares you also uproot the wheat with them.** Let both grow together **until the harvest**, and at the time of harvest I will say to the reapers, "First gather together the tares and bind them in bundles to burn them, but gather the wheat into my barn"

WHY THE RAPTURE?

THE FIRST COMING OF CHRIST WAS FOR THE SPIRIT

2 Cor 5:16-17

The first time Jesus came to the earth, and was born into this world he came to change mankind. It was through the first man Adam that sin entered the earth and changed man from life to death. It was Jesus who came as the last Adam, and changed man from death to life.

Your spirit was re-created and join to the spirit of God. You became the righteousness of God in Christ, but only in your spirit and not in your body. Through your soul you can determine that the spirit dominates the body, or that the body dominates the spirit. The one that wins is the one that you walk in the most. Before we are prepared for heaven the body is considered the flesh. If you are carnally minded you walk in the flesh. We have to walk in the spirit, and be spiritually minded in order for our bodies to be changed when we see Jesus.

BEING SPIRIT MINDED BRINGS LIFE

Romans 8:5-8
When a person lives after the flesh it means that he has limitations and cannot live a spiritual life. His mind is on things of the flesh. He is what we call carnally minded and is headed for death, but the spiritually minded is headed towards life and peace. The carnal mind is an enemy against God: because it is not subject to the law of God, and cannot please God.

SPIRIT IS LIFE. THE BODY WAS ADOPTED

Romans 8:14-16
if you are part of this body of believers is because you were changed when you became born-again. Your body was not changed or you would look different, but your spirit has been reborn, so God of adopted your body. Through the spirit of adoption we cry Abba our father, but the spirit bears witness with our spirit that we are the children of God. That means the Holy Spirit sees us as sons of God, but the body had to be adopted. There will be a day when we meet in the air, that we will be changed and given a glorified body to match our spirit.

YOU ARE A SON OR DAUGHTER OF GOD

John 1:12
If you have received Jesus, then you are a part of his family and have been given power to become a son of God.

THE RAPTURE IS FOR THE BODY

1 John 3:2-3 (NKJV) Beloved, now we are children of God; and it has not yet been revealed what we shall be, but we know that when He is revealed, <u>we shall be like Him, for we shall see Him as He is. And everyone who has this hope in Him purifies himself, just as He is pure.</u>

WHY THE RAPTURE?

THE FALLING AWAY

2O16 - presently there are approximately 300,000 who call themselves Christians, that are leaving Christianity.

2016 – there are 15,000 pastors leaving the vocation, of pastoring

2014 – as of this year in the United States Islam is growing at a faster rate than Christianity

FALLING AWAY AND THEN THE MAN OF SIN

2 Thess 2:2-3 (NKJV) Let no one deceive you by any means; for that Day will not come unless the falling away comes first, and the man of sin is revealed, the son of perdition,

To fulfill the falling away

The day of the Lord is coming and it shall not come in Mr.'s first a falling away. And while there is a falling away the son of perdition will be revealed. You will know him because he opposes God and Jesus his son and exalted himself attempting to show that he is God. He will be revealed at this time for the mystery of iniquity is already working, and when the Holy Spirit decides to no longer restrain and take himself out of the way then the wicked one will be revealed whom the Lord shall consume with the spirit of his mouth and shall destroy with the brightness of his coming.

WHY THE RAPTURE?

<u>TO REVEAL THE MYSTERY OF INIQUITY</u>
THE HOLY SPIRIT MUST FIRST BE TAKEN OUT OF THE WAY

2 Thess 2:6-7 (KJV) For the mystery of iniquity doth already work: only he who now letteth will let, until he be taken out of the way. *For the mystery of iniquity to be revealed, the Holy Spirit must leave this earth or as scripture says, he must be taken out of the way. Out of the way of what? **Out of the way of sin.** He is restraining sin. So are we if we are the salt of the earth. We will go with him.*

The Holy Spirit is holding back the totality of sin and degredation
THE MYSTERY OF INIQUITY IS ALREADY WORKING IN THE EARTH, BUT SOON SHALL BE REVEALED ONE OF THE PRIMARIES. THE ANTICHRIST, THE SON OF PERDITION. WE HAVE HEARD SO MUCH ABOUT.

A SIGNIFICATE SIGN

THE MAN OF SIN

According To Paul this "man of lawlessness" will oppose and **exalt himself above every so-called god**, and he will take the seat in the temple of God, in reference to the abomination of desolation.

There is much debate to whether the seventieth week immediately followed the sixty-ninth week, or the seventieth week commences at another time such as the tribulation.

If the seventieth week continued immediately after the sixty-ninth week, then it would have ended seven years after Christ's death. **AND IT DIDN'T ;** or the seventieth week could have continued through the destruction of the temple by Titus in A.D. 70, **but IT DIDN'T, BECAUSE**, there were things that weren't fulfilled in the description of the seventieth week. The main example, was in the gospel of Matthew, when Jesus alluded to the **"ABOMINATION OF DESOLATION"** which was spoken of by Daniel the prophet..." (Matthew 24:15) in reference to the time of the Great Tribulation (Matthew 24:21). There is the other part of Matthew where Jesus says "Immediately after the tribulation of those days"(verse29).

WHY THE RAPTURE?

TO REVEAL THIS MAN OF SIN

THE MAN OF SIN

As further illustrated, **the Anti-christ will pollute the sanctuary** and will take away the daily sacrifice, and they will do the abomination that causes desolation. And the Anti-christ will flatter or seduce (and deceive) those who hate the covenant. Daniel continues further:

"And the king shall do according to his will; and he shall exalt himself, and magnify himself above every god, and shall speak marvelous things against the God of gods, and shall prosper till the indignation be accomplished: for that is determined shall be done."

WHY THE RAPTURE?

So that prophecy may be fulfilled

THE MAN OF SIN

The king will do according to his own will, and he will exalt himself and he will place himself above every god. And He will speak great things against God. This king will prosper until the indignation is completed. Paul, in his second letter to the Thessalonians describes the man of lawlessness:

Dan 11:16 (KJV) But **he that cometh against him shall do according to his own will,** and none shall stand before him: and he shall stand in the glorious land, which by his hand shall be consumed

2nd Thessalonians 2:3-4
"Let no man deceive you by any means: for that day shall not come, except there come a falling away first, and that man of sin be revealed, the son of perdition; Who opposeth and exalteth himself above all that is called God, or that is worshipped; so that he as God sitteth in the temple of God, shewing himself that he is God."

The Tribulation

* THE TIME OF JACOBS TROUBLE

It was prophesied that Israel was to go into captivity for 70 years. It is recorded that Israel only search for 69 years the anger of the Lord required 70 years so one year which is called a week in Scripture was placed in the end times and called the time of Jacobs trouble. *The time of Jacobs trouble is what we call the tribulation.*

WHY THE RAPTURE?

THE TEMPLE MUST BE REBUILT
Another topic of debate concerns the temple itself. Will there be a tribulation without the temple? Remember in Daniel and 2 Thessalonians, the Lawless One will pollute the temple and will sit on God's throne; so the temple must be rebuilt in order for these things to commence.

HOWEVER THE TEMPLE NOT BEING BUILT, CANNOT STOP THE RAPTURE FROM TAKING PLACE.

JESUS GAVE HIS LIFE FOR HIS FUTURE BRIDE. HER JOB IS TO PREPARE AND AWAIT HIS RETURN

Matt 25:1-13 (KJV) Then shall the kingdom of heaven be likened unto ten virgins, which took their lamps, and went forth to meet the bridegroom. And five of them were wise, and five were foolish. They that were foolish took their lamps, and **took no oil** with them**: But the wise took oil in their vessels with their lamps.** While the bridegroom tarried, they all slumbered and slept. And at midnight there was a cry made, Behold, the bridegroom cometh; go ye out to meet him. Then all those virgins arose, and **trimmed their lamps**. And the foolish said unto the wise, Give us of your oil; for our lamps are gone out. But the wise answered, saying, Not so; lest there be not enough for us and you: but **go ye rather to them that sell, and buy for yourselves.** And while they went to buy, the bridegroom came; and they that were ready went in with him to the marriage: and the door was shut. Afterward came also the other virgins, saying, Lord, Lord, open to us. But he answered and said, Verily I say unto you, I know you not. **Watch therefore, for ye know neither the day nor the hour wherein the Son of man cometh.**

WHY THE RAPTURE?

SO HIS SON CAN BE WED

GOD DESIRES A WIFE FOR HIS SON

ABOUT THE BRIDE

Just as Abraham desired a wife for Isaac and one of his kin.
Just as the servant of Abraham went into the far country to find a kinsman to the wife of his son, so did the Holy Spirit coming to the earth to find those

who were willing to return with him, and to find a wife for the son of the one who sent him. Notice the father sent his servant for the son.

REBEKAH WAS ESPOUSED TO ISAAC

ABOUT THE BRIDE
Gen 24:2-7

Abraham made his eldest servant swear by the Lord, the God of heaven, and the God of earth, that he should not take a wife for Isaac his son out of the daughters of the Canaanites. He made them swear that he would go into the Abraham's kindred and take a wife of his kindred. Eliezer's question was what if I go into this country and the woman wants to use see what Isaac looks like see if they're compatible. In other words what if she's not willing to come should I take Isaac into this far country that they they may see who he is and how he is. Abraham said no; you must not take my son into this land again. If she does not come your free from the oath.

YOU ARE JESUS KINDRED / he wants a wife of his kindred THE HOLY SPIRIT PREDETERMINED WHAT SHE IS TO DO / he says if she is to refresh him. Make his journey lighter then she is the one.

The church is Jesus's kindred. We are his brothers and sisters. We are in the far country from which he has come, and the Holy Spirit was sent among Jesus's people to return with the bride. When he finds the one that qualifies, and when the father tells Jesus to go get his bride, it will be time for that bride to leave this earth with the Holy Spirit, just as Rebecca left the city of Nahor to go with Eliezer to Isaac.

THE CHURCH IS ESPOUSED TO CHRIST

ABOUT THE BRIDE

2 Cor 11:2 (KJV) For I am jealous over you with godly jealousy: for I have espoused you to one husband, that I may present you as a chaste virgin to Christ.

But you are made a part of his body. Christ has made you bone of his bone, and flesh of his flesh and he did it to save your life and to redeem the Pearl that he found of great price, and make it his very own.

YOU ARE HIS PEARL OF GREAT PRICE

ABOUT THE CHURCH

Matt 13:44-46
Jesus gave a parable in which he said the kingdom of heaven is like treasure hidden in a field and when a man has found this treasure he hides it. He so happy that he found this treasure that he goes back and sells everything that he has to buy that field.

We the church are the hidden treasure. The world cannot see when we are born again. The world cannot see that our spirit has been changed. The man Jesus has found the treasure and this is how it was hidden. The world cannot see it is a treasure. Jesus gave his life to buy that field which is the whole earth, he gave all that he had to purchase not just field but the treasure as well.

WHY THE RAPTURE?

OUR BODY IS THE TEMPLE OF THE HOLY SPIRIT

ABOUT THE CHURCH

WE'VE EXPERIENCED THE EARTHLY; NOW FOR THE HEAVENLY

1 Cor 15:49
It is such a wonderful thing that even though all we have ever known is the earthly, that one day we shall know the heavenly.

*IN THE EARTH WE ARE ALWAYS MARRIED TO AN EARTHLY SPOUSE, BUT IN OUR FINISHED STATE WHICH IS ETERNAL WE MUST BE LIKE OUR HEAVENLY SPOUSE, WHICH IS CHRIST.

ABOUT THE CHURCH

1 Cor 6:17-20 (KJV) Flee fornication. Every sin that a man doeth is without the body; but he that committeth fornication sinneth against his own body. What? know ye not that your body is the temple of the Holy Ghost which is in you, which ye have of God, and ye are not your own? **For ye are bought with a price: therefore** glorify God in your body, and in your spirit, which are God's.

YOU BELONG IN HEAVEN BECAUSE

YOU WERE BOUGHT WITH A GREAT PRICE

ABOUT THE CHURCH

You are bought with a price. Jesus is the merchant who went into a far country. He was looking for a good Pearl and he found one in you. He sold all that he had to purchase you. Satan hates you, because you are made in the image of God. Is it any wonder he is trying to accumulate as many souls as possible? He is buying souls to send them to hell where he can torment them for looking like God.

YOU ARE THE BETROTHED

TO ONE WHO IS IN HEAVEN

To be betrothal to Jesus Christ he has laid down the dowry which was his life. He has given you the Holy Spirit which is in earnest or a guarantee for your inheritance. He has given you to drink from the cup of salvation to validate your future marriage.

WE WERE PURCHASED

ABOUT THE CHURCH

You were purchased for a price

1 Cor 7:23-24 (KJV) Ye are bought with a price; be not ye the servants of men. Brethren, let every man, wherein he is called, therein abide with God.

You were not purchased with corruptible things

1 Peter 1:18-19 (NKJV) knowing that you were not redeemed with corruptible things, like silver or gold, from your aimless conduct received by tradition from your fathers, but with the precious blood of Christ, as of a lamb without blemish and without spot.

REDEEMED BY THE BLOOD OF THE LAMB

ABOUT THE CHURCH

1 Peter 1:17-19 (KJV) Forasmuch as ye know that ye were not redeemed with corruptible things, as silver and gold, from your vain conversation received by tradition from your fathers; **19 But with the precious blood of Christ,** as of a lamb without blemish and without spot:

BOAZ; RUTHS KINDRED

ABOUT THE BRIDE

Ruth 3:1-2 (KJV) Then Naomi her mother in law said unto her, My daughter, shall I not seek rest for thee, that it may be well with thee? **And now, is not Boaz of our kindred,** with whose maidens thou wast? Behold, **he winnoweth barley to night in the threshing floor.**

We are of God. Jesus has purchased us and made us a new creature. We are in the God class, because he gave us power to become the sons of God.

WE ARE THOSE WHO OBEY HIM. WE WERE WINNOWED BY THE HOLY SPIRIT, and in the darkest of night.. THE WORD SPIRIT IN HEBREW IS THE A SAME AS WIND. THE CHAFF OF SIN WAS BLOWN OUT OF US, TO PREPARE US TO BE WITH JESUS.

YOU ARE OF GODS KINDRED

ABOUT THE CHURCH

John 1:12 (NKJV) But as many as received Him, to them He gave the right to become children of God, to those who believe in His name:

WINNOWED IN DARK TIMES

ABOUT THE BRIDE

Normally barley was to be __winnowed at night when the wind was right in order to toss it up so the Wind could blow the chaff away.__ We as Christians need to make an effort to allow the Holy Spirit to blow away the chaff of sin out of our lives that we may be suited for the bridegroom.

THESE ARE THE RAPTURED SAINTS / BARLEY

Ruth 3:2 (KJV) Behold, he winnoweth barley tonight in the threshing floor. *We are living in dark times and I believe barley is representative of those who are going in the rapture. We are being prepared by the Lord*.

I believe barley to be better winnowed at night and in the darkest hour. That's when the wind, spirit, Ruach Hachodesh can better get our attention. The word "wind" is the same as the word "spirit". It is the (holy) spirit that blows the sin out of our lives, just as the wind blows the chaff.

THESE ARE THE TRIBULATION SAINTS/WHEAT

I believe there are another group of Christians, who are better represented by the wheat.

Before the wheat harvest, the priest goes out into the field and takes a handful of wheat, offering it up before the Lord.

After offering the wheat before the Lord, the priest takes it to the temple, and offers a Lamb as sacrifice. Because he lifted it up, the firstfruits sanctified the whole field, but these Christians represented by the wheat are the hardheaded ones, the ones who are not doing the will of God, the ones who have no relationship with God, and forsake their fellowship with the Saints.

TRIBULATION SAINTS

The wheat harvest is symbolic of the tribulation Saints. Those who will miss the rapture because they are not ready, but during the tribulation they shall be made ready, for they shall learn to be willing to give all, even their very lives.

NOTE: the wheat is also processed; not by winnowing, but by crushing. The wheat must be crushed to discard the chaff or sin. The wheat is rolled over by a board attached to a mule. This board is called a tribulon. The tribulon crushes the wheat to make it ready.

Tribulon - sound familiar? / It sounds like what it represents – the tribulation

FACTS ABOUT THE END TIME WRATH OF GOD (TIME OF JACOBS TROUBLE)

DANIELS 70th WEEK (The tribulation)

Continuing further in our discussion, Daniel wrote a vital part of much importance:

"And they that understand among the people shall instruct many; yet they shall fall by the sword, and by flame, by captivity and by spoil, many days. Now when they shall fall, they shall be **holpen** with a little help; but many shall cleave to them with flatteries. And some of them of understanding shall fall, to try them, and to purge, and to make them white, even to the time of the end: because it is yet for a time appointed."

HOLPEN = helped
(Chapter 11 verses 33-35)
There are some who shall fall by the sword even though they have helped others and strengthen others, and given them hope, they themselves shall fall.

WHY THE RAPTURE?
YOU ARE GOD'S WATCHMAN
The sword is coming upon the land
I am blowing the trumpet

Ezek 33:3-9 (KJV)

If when he seeth the sword come upon the land, he blow <u>the trumpet</u>, and warn the people; **4 Then whosoever heareth the sound of the trumpet, and taketh not warning; if the sword come, and take him away, his blood shall be upon his own head**. **5** He heard the sound of the trumpet, and took not warning; his blood shall be upon him. But he that taketh warning shall deliver his soul. **6 But if the watchman see the sword come, and blow not the trumpet, and the people be not warned; if the sword come, and take *any* person from among them, he is taken away in his iniquity; but his blood will I require at the watchman's hand.** **7** So thou, O son of man, I have set thee a watchman unto the house of Israel; therefore thou shalt hear the word at my mouth, and warn them from me. **8 When I say unto the wicked, O wicked *man*, thou shalt surely die; if thou dost not speak to warn the wicked from his way, that wicked *man* shall die in his iniquity; but his blood will I require at thine hand.** **9** Nevertheless, if thou warn the wicked of his way to turn from it; if he do not turn from his way, he shall die in his iniquity; but thou hast delivered thy soul.

Because we are God's watchman our job is to populate heaven and depopulate hell. Why do we depopulate hell, because we don't want anybody to go there. Why do we populate heaven because that's where we were assigned for ever and we want other people to have the same benefit because that's the heart of the father.

THERE WILL BE PERSECUTION

In the above verses, There will be those who will understand and have insight about the king. They will instruct and warn many, but many will die by persecution for "many days." There will be many of these who will fall and they will be helped by those who will end up deceiving them with flatteries. Those others of the understanding will fall, some will be purified and go through the process "to make white" or be made righteous up to the time of the end.

THE TRIBULATION

MANY WILL FALL. MANY WILL NOT HAVE UNDERSTANDING AND INSIGHT AND SHALL BE DECEIVE BY FLATTERERS, AND BETRAYED.

Some will be cast into prison for 10 days
THIS IS JACOB'S TROUBLE/ NOT THE CHURCH

TO FULFILL DANIELS 70ᵗʰ WEEK
The vital part of the pre-tribulational view, the seventy weeks is for the "Jews only." Anything else does not concern the church because they weren't here for the sixty-nine weeks. And because they weren't here for those sixty-nine weeks, they won't be here for the seventieth either. Looking into the Gospel of Matthew, before Jesus' death on the cross (after the 69ᵗʰ week), Jesus said in reference to the church:

BE FAITHFUL UNTO DEATH

Rev 2:10-11 (NKJV) Do not fear any of those things which you are about to suffer. Indeed, the devil is about to throw some of you into prison, that you may be tested, and you will have tribulation ten days. Be faithful until death, and I will give you the crown of life. 11 He who has an ear, let him hear what the Spirit says to the churches. He who overcomes shall not be hurt by the second death."

You may go through the tribulation, but if you are faithful to the end you won't have to experience the second death which is in hell.

THERE ARE THREE GROUPS OF PEOPLE OF WHOM GOD SPEAKS TO IN THE BIBLE. THEY ARE THE JEWS, THE GENTILES AND THE CHRISTIANS.

IF YOU NOTICE, IN THE BOOK OF REVELATION GOD STOPPED SPEAKING TO THE CHRISTIANS AT THE END OF CHAPTER 3.

IT IS IN CHAPTER 3 THAT HE TELLS THE CHURCH OF PHILADELPHIA THAT BECAUSE OF THEIR OBEDIENCE AND PATIENCE, THEY WILL BE SPARED THE TRIAL THAT IS ABOUT TO COME UPON THE WHOLE EARTH. And then nothing else about the church; as if revelations 4:1 when it says come up hither, the church is taken up hither. This looks like the rapture. There is no more mention of the church except the tribulation Saints

I WILL KEEP THEE, (YOU WILL BE RAPTURED)

Rev 3:10 (KJV) Because you have kept the word of my patience, I also will keep you from the hour of temptation, which shall come upon all the world, to try them that dwell upon the earth.

COME UP HITHER

This fourth chapter of revelations ends the presence of the bride upon the earth.
I BELEIVE JOHN WHO IS A PART OF THE CHURCH WAS TOLD TO **COME UP HITHER.** *(I BELEIVE THIS IS A METAPHOR FOR THE RAPTURE)*

Rev 4:1 (KJV) After this I looked, and, behold, a door was opened in heaven: and the first voice which I heard was as it were of a trumpet talking with me; which said, **Come up hither, and I will shew thee things which must be hereafter.**

THINGS THAT WILL COME AFTER WHAT? THE RAPTURE; AFTER YOU COME UP HITHER, I'LL SHOW YOU WHAT IS TO COME AFTER YOU COME UP HERE AND ARE RAPTURED.

WHY THE RAPTURE?

OR WHAT IS ITS PURPOSE
TO RECEIVE THE SAINTS UNTO HIMSELF

John 14:1-3
This is the ultimate promise. The promises starts out with comforting words let not your heart be troubled you believe in God believe also in me. As you see this message is directed to the believing one's. Jesus says in my father's house are many mansions, if it were not so, I would've told you I go and prepare a place for you, I will come again, and receive you unto myself; that where I am, there you may be also.

*Our ultimate goal as a church is to receive Jesus Christ as our King and Lord, and especially as the bridegroom. Churches throughout the ages have had one focus and that is to go to heaven. Jesus wants us there and has prepared to receive some of us, through the rapture.

JESUS IS GLORIOUS

He is to receive a glorious church
Eph 5:27 (KJV) <u>That he might present it to himself a glorious church, not having spot, or wrinkle, or any such thing; but that it should be holy and without blemish.</u>
BE HOLY FOR I AM HOLY

YOU' VE BEEN GIVEN TIME TO PREPARE FOR THE WEDDING

Jesus gave us time as the bride of Christ to prepare for his return. To prepare means to get the sin out, and the only way to do that is to have our lamps full so that we may see.

You cannot read the word without light on the word. You must be filled, your lamps must be trimmed and lit that you may find your way to him.

What good is a lamp with no oil? You are going to need the holy spirit to go get illumination to see your way to Jesus.
When Jesus comes there will be a gathering

2 Thess 2:1 (KJV) Now we beseech you, brethren, <u>by the coming of our Lord Jesus Christ, and</u> **by our gathering together unto him,**

GATHERING TOGETHER = EPISUNAGOGE
EPISUNAGOGE = means Christ himself is the object of this assembly. (This passage is used only one time in the Bible)

We will be meeting with Christ one time. There are however other passages of the Bible that speak of a gathering, but a different word in a different meaning is expressed.

THE DAY OF CHRIST IS AT HAND

EPISUNAGOGE
2 Thess 2:1-2 (KJV)
1 Now we beseech you, brethren, by the coming of our Lord Jesus Christ, **and *by* our gathering together unto him,** **2** That ye be not soon shaken in mind, or be troubled, neither by spirit, nor by word, nor by letter as from us, as that **the day of Christ is at hand.**

GATHERING TOGETHER = EPISUNAGOGE
EPISUNAGOGE = a gathering, or collection, an assembly together at one place. An assembly for corporate worship, not as an occasion but as customary conduct. This is a gathering of something very valuable to Christ.

*<u>**The day of Christ**</u> is a glorious day for all of the righteous. Christ is to be the center of **EPISUNAGOGE**. This day of Christ is not the day of the Lord. This is a happy gathering for God the Father, God the son, God the Holy Spirit, The Bride of Christ, and the Angels.*

__The day of the Lord__ is judgement day
Mal 4:3-4 (NKJV) You shall trample the wicked,
For they shall be ashes under the soles of your feet
On the day that I do this,"
Says the Lord of hosts.

The custom of heaven

*We have a Christ who is awaiting the opportunity to gather us together, to collect us, to assemble us for the purpose of cultural worship. Cultural worship is the custom of heaven.

Christ would never separate himself from us because of the dread of persecution, and __we should not separate ourselves from Him for the dread of persecution,__ but remain faithful unto the end.

WHY THE RAPTURE?

JESUS will never **EGKATALEIPO**

EGKATALEIPO = To desert or leave stranded, to leave neglected, give up, or abandon. It is the mere avoidance of assembling for religious worship. To separate oneself from the local Christians because of the dread of persecution.

CHRIST WILL NOT DESERT YOU OR LEAVE YOU
Heb 13:5 (KJV) *Let your* conversation *be* without covetousness; *and be* content with such things as ye have: for he hath said, **I will never leave thee, nor forsake thee.**

DEMAS FORSOOK PAUL (**EGKATALEIPO**)

2 Tim 4:10-11 (NKJV) for Demas has forsaken me, having loved this present world, and has departed for Thessalonica--Crescens for Galatia, Titus for Dalmatia. 11 Only Luke is with me.

CHRIST WILL NEVER FORSAKE US. HE WILL NEVER **EGKATALEIPO** US. **WE MUST NEVER FORSAKE HIM.**

THE FATHER TURNED AWAY FROM HIS SON, BECAUSE HE (THE FATHER) IS HOLY AND COULD NOT LOOK UPON OUR SIN LAID UPON JESUS.

Here's the same word is used **EGKATALEIPO**

EGKATALEIPO - forsaken

Mark 15:34 (NKJV) And at the ninth hour Jesus cried out with a loud voice, saying, "Eloi, Eloi, lama sabachthani?" which is translated, "My God, My God, why have You forsaken Me?"

TO TOTALLY END INFIRMITIES

Heb 2:17-18
*because the sin that the world had accumulated sent Jesus to the cross and caused him to be treated as he was treated, he can bear your infirmities.

This Scripture says that in all things Jesus had to be made like his brethren, speaking of us and it was for the purpose that he might be a merciful and faithful high priest in all things pertaining to God to be made a propitiation for the sins of the people. For in that he himself has suffered, and have been tempted, he is able to aid those who are tempted.

BE FAITHFUL UNTIL DEATH

Rev 2:10 (NKJV) Do not fear any of those things which you are about to suffer. Indeed, the devil is about to throw **some of you into prison**, that you may be tested, and you will have tribulation ten days. **Be faithful until death**, and I will give you the crown of life. **SOME OF YOU, NOT ALL OF YOU. - SOME WILL ESCAPE THIS.**

EVERY MAN IN HIS OWN ORDER

1 Cor 15:23-27

Even though Enoch went to heaven without dying, Elijah went to heaven without dying none of them could of gone without the resurrection of Christ. Even though Jesus resurrection was much later without his rising from the dead, none of the other resurrections would've taken place. Christ is the firstfruits; I say this because in the days of old a person would go out for the first harvests of the field and pluck a handful of barley or wheat and raise it before the Lord waving it as a wave offering and then he would take it to the priest who would blessed and slay a Lamb to declare the first of the harvest holy. This sanctified the whole field because the first was risen up. Jesus is the first of the harvest, afterwards we that are at crisis coming, and then comes the end.

TO BE MADE HOLY

HE WANTS US HOLY; FOR HE IS HOLY

Christ is the firstfruits. This means that he is the sanctifier of the whole field. The priest would go out before the barley or the wheat harvest, he would take a handful of the firstfruits of the harvest and would wave it before God and proclaim the whole field, sanctified, and holy. Then the priest would return to the Temple and make a sacrifice. Christ has sanctified the Saints because he is a type of firstfruits. The firstfruits have been plucked and offered to God the father, and now we remain, and then will come the end.

HE WANTS US IMMORTAL AND INCORRUPTIBLE

1 COR 15:51 *But thanks be to God, which giveth us the victory through our Lord Jesus Christ.*

At the last Trump we shall be changed. We shall be changed in the twinkling of an eye. Our bodies shall be transformed into glorious bodies. We do not know what we will be, or what we will be like, but we know that when we see him, we will be changed to be like him.

OH, JUST TO BE LIKE JESUS (YESHUA)

TO BE LIKE HIM

1 John 3:2-3 Beloved, now we are children of God; and it has not yet been revealed what we shall be, but we know that when He is revealed, we shall be like Him, for we shall see Him as He is.

WHY THE RAPTURE?

THE RAPTURE BLESSES THE SAINTS

The first resurrection saints are blessed

Phil 3:10-11 (KJV) If by any means I might **attain unto the resurrection of the dead.**

DEAD = Nekros / naturally dead or death of the body

This means to be one of the dead in Christ shall rise as mentioned in first Thessalonians 4:16, 17 where is mentioned that the dead in Christ shall rise first.

2 Cor 5:6-10

We are confident actually in knowing that once we leave this vile body life truly begins for to be absent from the body is to be present with the Lord. And I know that we walk by faith and not by sight but because we trust him and because of what he placed in us an earnest of the promise an earnest for our inheritance the Holy Spirit is a guarantee that we will be with Jesus saw are labor is that we may be accepted of him and that we may appear before the judgment seat of Christ: scratch that; that every one may receive the things done in his body what he's done rather good or bad.

WHY THE RAPTURE?

TO CHANGE OUR VILE BODIES

Phil 3:20-21

We shall receive a glorious body. 1 john 3:3 says that we do not know what we will be but we know that we will be like him when he appears because we will see him as he is. This vile body we will put off, and the glorious body we will put on

THAT WE MAY BE
CLOTHED WITH A HEAVENLY TABERNACLE
2 Cor 5:1-8

This Scripture is actually saying that if something should happen to this earthly body, knowing that we are eternal beings we will no longer be housed by a building of clay, but by a tabernacle of heaven. We yearn for this house of heaven that we may be close with the eternal tabernacle for we know that if we are close we will not be found naked so we continue to be obedient to the word of God.

TO END YOUR LABOR
ABOUND IN THE WORK OF THE LORD
1 Cor 15:51-58

We know the many benefits of being steadfast, unmovable, always abounding in the work of the Lord, because our works is not in vain we have a short time in the earth but eternal life is forever. Just to understand that only what you do for Christ will last is the greatest motivator.

DON'T SORROW OVER THE DEAD IN CHRIST

1 Thess 4:13 (KJV) But I would not have you to be ignorant, brethren, concerning them which are asleep, that ye sorrow not, even as others which have no hope. You have a hope. You will see those who have died in Christ again.

OUR LOVED ONES ARE WITH HIM NOW

1 Thess 4:16-18 (NKJV) For the Lord Himself will descend from heaven with a shout, with the voice of an archangel, and with the trumpet of God. And the dead in Christ will rise first. 17 Then we who are alive and remain shall be caught up together with them in the clouds to meet the Lord in the air. And thus we shall always be with the Lord. **18 Therefore comfort one another with these words.**

WE WILL ONCE AGAIN BE UNITED WITH OUR LOVED ONES

WE ARE CONFIDENT, YES

2 Cor 5:7-8 (NKJV) 8 We are confident, yes, well pleased rather **to be absent from the body and to be present with the Lord.**

WHY THE RAPTURE?

TO BRING OUR LOVED ONES WITH HIM

1 Thess 4:17-18 (NKJV) Therefore comfort one another with these words.

*YOU HAVE A HOPE. IT'S CALLED THE BLESSED HOPE. IF YOU SORROW IT'S NOT BECAUSE JESUS IS UNFAITHFUL, BUT BECAUSE YOU ARE THINKING IN FEAR AND NOT HOPE.

THE LORD WANTS YOU TO TRUST HIM.

QUESTION: HOW CAN WE TRUST HIM?
ANSWER: BY HOPING IN JESUS AND DOING THINGS TO MAKE YOUR ELECTION SURE.
OUR HOPE IS :

HE IS THE BLESSED HOPE

Titus 2:13-14 (NKJV) looking for the blessed hope and glorious appearing of our great God and Savior Jesus Christ, 14 who gave Himself for us, that He might redeem us from every lawless deed and purify for Himself His own special people, zealous for good works.

THE THINGS TO MAKE OUR ELECTION SURE ARE:

2 Peter 1:5-11 (KJV) And beside this, giving all diligence, add to your faith virtue; and to virtue knowledge; 6 And to knowledge temperance; and to temperance patience; and to patience godliness; 7 And to godliness brotherly kindness; and to brotherly kindness charity. 8 For if these things be in you, and abound, they make you that ye shall neither be barren nor unfruitful in the knowledge of our Lord Jesus Christ. 9 But he that lacketh these things is blind, and cannot see afar off, and hath forgotten that he was purged from his old sins. 10 Wherefore the rather, brethren, **give diligence to make your calling and election sure:** for if ye do these things, ye shall never fall: 11 For so an entrance shall be ministered unto you abundantly into the everlasting kingdom of our Lord and Saviour Jesus Christ.

THAT HE MAY BRING THE DEAD IN CHRIST WITH HIM?

1 Thess 4:13-18 (KJV) But I would not have you to be ignorant, brethren, concerning them which are asleep, that ye sorrow not, even as others which have no hope. **14 For if we believe that Jesus died and rose again, even so them also which sleep in Jesus will God bring with him.** 15 For this we say unto you by the word of the Lord, that we which are alive and remain unto the coming of the Lord shall not prevent them which are asleep. 16 For the Lord himself shall descend from heaven with a shout, with the voice of the archangel, and with the trump of God: and the dead in Christ shall rise first: 17 Then we which are alive and remain shall be caught up together with them in the clouds, to meet the Lord in the air: and so shall we ever be with the Lord**. 18 Wherefore comfort one another with these words.**

DO YOU BELIEVE JESUS DIED AND ROSE AGAIN? IF SO KNOW THEN THAT HE WILL BRING YOUR RELATIVES WITH HIM.

WE ARE TO COMFORT EACH OTHER WITH THESE WORDS

THAT HE MAY BRING THE DEAD IN CHRIST WITH HIM
*Understand that those who die in Christ are with him in heaven. **How else could he bring them with him when he comes.***

WHY THE RAPTURE?

THAT WE MAY BE PRESENT WITH THE LORD

2 Cor 5:8 (KJV) We are confident, I say, and willing rather **to be absent from the body**, and **to be present with the Lord.**

**TO BE ABSENT FROM THE BODY IS TO BE PRESENT WITH THE LORD*

*In the word of God it says **to be absent from the body is to be present with the Lord.** They are present with the Lord and when Jesus returns they will be with him. They will come and pick up their bodies and be glorified. And we which remain shall be changed, and caught up to be with Christ in the air.*

WHY THE RAPTURE?

THE RAPTURE WILL MAKE A DIFFERENCE BETWEEN THE MARK OF GOD AND THE MARK OF THE BEAST

Rev 20:1-4 (KJV) And I saw an angel come down from heaven, having the key of the bottomless pit and a great chain in his hand. 2 And he laid hold on the dragon, that old serpent, which is the Devil, and Satan, and bound him a thousand years, 3 And cast him into the bottomless pit, and shut him up, and set a seal upon him, that he should deceive the nations no more, till the thousand years should be fulfilled: and after that he must be loosed a little season. 4 And I saw thrones, and they sat upon them, and judgment was given unto them: **and I saw the souls of them that were beheaded for the witness of Jesus, and for the word of God, and which had not worshipped the beast, neither his image, neither had received his mark upon their foreheads, or in their hands; and they lived and reigned with Christ a thousand years.**

Example of God's mark:

Rev 7:2-3
And I saw another angel ascending from the east, having the seal of the living God: and he cried with a loud voice to the four angels, to whom it was given to hurt the earth and the sea, **3** Saying, Hurt not the earth, neither the sea, nor the trees, **till we have sealed the servants of our God in their foreheads**.

Example of satan's mark:

Rev 13:16-17
And he causeth all, both small and great, rich and poor, free and bond, **to receive a mark in their right hand, or in their foreheads:** **17** And that no man might buy or sell, save he that had the mark, or the name of the beast, or the number of his name

That we may receive Reward and Blessing

John 14:1-3 (KJV) **To take the Saints to heaven where they will receive judgment for works done in the body, receive the rewards, and partake of the marriage supper.**1 Let not your heart be troubled: ye believe in God, believe also in me. 2 In my Father's house are many mansions: if it were not so, I would have told you. I go to prepare a place for you. 3 And if I go and prepare a place for you, I will come again, and receive you unto myself; that where I am, there ye may be also.

Can you imagine?

Can you imagine going to heaven, and not receiving punishment for the evil works that were done in our body, but instead receiving rewards for what we should have done anyway to honor the one who saved us, and raised us? Can you imagine being betrothed to this saviour who loves us so, and being invited to then partake of a wedding that He has prepared for us which gives us glory unspeakable? **Can you imagine?**

WHY THE RAPTURE?

FOR US TO APPEAR WITH HIM IN GLORY

Col 3:4 (KJV) When Christ, who is our life, shall appear, then shall ye also appear with him in glory.

THAT OUR HEARTS MAY BE ESTABLISHED HOLY

1 Thess 3:13 (KJV) To the end he may stablish your hearts unblameable in holiness before God, even our Father, at the coming of our Lord Jesus Christ with all his saints.

*STABLISH = **Histemi** / to set firmly and permanently. To establish, and to confirm. To establish us unblamable in holiness before God.*

He's establishing your heart unblamable before God

*The Scripture means Christ will still be working on you, and establishing your heart unblamable in holiness before God, even up to the return of Christ.

WHY THE RAPTURE?

THAT WE MAY APPEAR BEFORE THE JUDGEMENT SEAT TO RECEIVE DONE UNTO OUR BODIES, ACCORDING TO OUR WORKS

2 Cor 5:10 (KJV) For we must all appear before the judgment seat of Christ; that every one may receive the things done in his body, according to that he hath done, whether it be good or bad.

And after these things I heard a great voice of much people in heaven, saying, Alleluia; Salvation, and glory, and honour, and power, unto the Lord our God:

WHY THE RAPTURE?

THAT THE CHURCH MAY BE CALLED TO THE MARRIAGE SUPPER OF THE LAMB

And a voice came out of the throne, saying, Praise our God, all ye his servants, and ye that fear him, both small and great. And I heard as it were the voice of a great multitude, and as the voice of many waters, and as the voice of mighty thunderings, saying, Alleluia: for the Lord God omnipotent reigneth. Let us be glad and rejoice, and give honour to him: for the marriage of the Lamb is come, and his wife hath made herself ready. And to her was granted that she should be arrayed in fine linen, clean and white: for the fine linen is the righteousness of saints. And he saith unto me, Write**, Blessed are they which are called unto the marriage supper of the Lamb.** And he saith unto me, These are the true sayings of God. And I fell at his feet to worship him. And he said unto me, See thou do it not: I am thy fellowservant, and of thy brethren that have the testimony of Jesus: worship God: for the testimony of Jesus is the spirit of prophecy.

To present the Saints as perfect before God the Father and to be forever with him

Col 1:28-29 (NKJV) Him we preach, warning every man and teaching every man in all wisdom**, that we may present every man perfect in Christ Jesus.** 29 To this end I also labor, striving according to His working which works in me mightily.

PERFECT = Teleiotes / fully grown. Having been perfected. Having achieved the goal and being eligible for the prize.

WHY THE RAPTURE?

To fulfill the day of Christ

2 Thess 2:1-2 (KJV) Now we beseech you, brethren, by the coming of our Lord Jesus Christ, and by our gathering together unto him, That ye be not soon shaken in mind, or be troubled, neither by spirit, nor by word, nor by letter as from us, as that the day of Christ is at hand.

This word gathering is the word – EPISUNAGOGE

EPISUNAGOGE – Not avoiding the responsibility that it takes to be with Christ and other believers. Not betraying one's attachment to Christ. This refers to separating oneself from the local Christian community because of the dread of persecution. This refers to Christ himself as the one to which the assembly was attached.

TO HAVE THE COURAGE TO STAND WITH CHRIST

WHY THE RAPTURE?
To make the Saints whole: body, soul, and spirit
1 Thess 5:23 (KJV) And the very God of peace sanctify you wholly; and I pray God your whole spirit and soul and body be preserved blameless unto the coming of our Lord Jesus Christ.

To put an end to potential weariness
2 Thess 3:13 (KJV) But ye, brethren, be not weary in well doing.

To put an end to weariness and fainting
Gal 6:8-9 (KJV) And let us not be weary in well doing: for in due season we shall reap, if we faint not.

To receive the fruit of the early and latter rain.
James 5:7 (KJV) Be patient therefore, brethren, unto the coming of the Lord. Behold, the husbandman waiteth for the precious fruit of

the earth, and hath long patience for it, <u>until he receive the early and latter rain.</u>

To cause the Saints to escape the tribulation and all these things, and stand before the Son of Man

Luke 21:33-36 (KJV) And take heed to yourselves, lest at any time your hearts be overcharged with surfeiting, and drunkenness, and cares of this life, and so that day come upon you unawares. 35 For as a snare shall it come on all them that dwell on the face of the whole earth. **<u>36 Watch ye therefore, and pray always, that ye may be accounted worthy to escape all these things that shall come to pass, and to stand before the Son of man. As the days of Noah so shall the coming of the Son of Man be</u>**

To fulfill the word of God
Noah went into the Ark before the flood came
Luke 17:26 (KJV) And as it was in the days of Noe, so shall it be also in the days of the Son of man.

The Holy Spirit will no longer restrain sin

All hell will break loose in the earth

He who now restrains will no longer restrain. The restrainer is the Holy Spirit, and once he takes the church to heaven he will no longer be on earth to hold back Sin. That is why the wicked man will be revealed.

The Holy Spirit is the restrainer, and because of the future raptured Saints, the Holy Spirit will take the salt of the earth out of the earth and allow iniquity to take its course.

To reveal that his church is not the object of wrath
1 Thess 5:9 (KJV) For God hath not appointed us to wrath, but to obtain salvation by our Lord Jesus Christ,
Yeshua (Jesus) is not mad at you

WHY THE RAPTURE?

TO BEGIN THE TRIBULATION

__For me to better emphasize the purpose of the rapture, I would not do it justice unless I also explained the purpose of the tribulation.__

You must first understand that the tribulation is not for the church, but for Israel. That is why it is called Daniel's 70th week, and the time of Jacob's trouble.

Many of the false teachers teach without understanding the principles that God has shown in his word. He is not designed us for wrath, and he is able to deliver the godly.

As he did for Noah, and as he did for Lot he will do for you.

WHY THE RAPTURE?

TO BRING FORTH THE TRIBULATION

THE PURPOSE OF THE TRIBULATION

Jacobs trouble, the wrath of God, Daniels 70th week. These are all terms for the tribulation

<u>To purify Israel and bring it back to a place where God can fulfill the everlasting covenants made with their fathers.</u>

WHY THE RAPTURE?

WHY THE TRIBULATION?

To judge Israel and to punish them for their rejection of the Messiah and to make them willing to accept him when he comes the second time.

<u>To bring Israel to complete repentance</u>

*Is it so hard to understand that the tribulation is part of this last chastening of the Jewish people. The Jews went into captivity because of their disobedience, but only fullfilled 69 weeks of that captivity. They owe God one more week (7 years), of their punishment which is to take place now. This week is called the tribulation.

TO SEE WHO THEY HAVE PIERCED

Zech 12:10
God will pour out on the house of David the inhabitants of Jerusalem the spirit of grace and supplication. This spirit of grace is God giving them what they don't deserve, nor can they repay for this grace. After this grace is poured out they will be blessed that their eyes are opened and they shall look upon Jesus whom they have pierced, yes they will mourn for him whom mourns for his only son and grieve for him as one grieves for a firstborn. For the first time they will see that he is truly the Messiah, the son of God.

THE GREAT DAY OF THE LORD

Mal 4:3-4 (NKJV) You shall trample the wicked,
For they shall be ashes under the soles of your feet
On the day that I do this,"
Says the Lord of hosts.

"Remember the Law of Moses, My servant,
Which I commanded him in Horeb for all Israel,
With the statutes and judgments.

WHY THE RAPTURE?

WHY THE TRIBULATION?

To judge Israel and to punish them for their rejection of the Messiah and to make them willing to accept him when he comes the second time.

ISRAEL'S CONTINUED REBELLION

Ezek 20:33-34 The Lord God says surely with a mighty hand and outstretched arm, and with fury poured out, I will rule over you. I will bring you out from the peoples and gather you out of the countries where you are scattered with a mighty hand, with an outstretched arm, and a fury poured out. God will call his people out of the countries where they are scattered and bring them back to Israel.

THIS IS MY PEOPLE

Zech 13:9 (NKJV) I will bring the one-third through the fire,
Will refine them as silver is refined,
And test them as gold is tested.
They will call on My name,
And I will answer them.
I will say, 'This is My people';
And each one will say, 'The Lord is my God.'

THE COMING OF THE LORD

Zech 14:1-15 (NKJV) Behold, the day of the Lord is coming,
And your spoil will be divided in your midst.
For I will gather all the nations to battle against Jerusalem;

The city shall be taken, The houses rifled, And the women ravished.
Half of the city shall go into captivity,
But the remnant of the people shall not be cut off from the city.
Then the Lord will go forth
And fight against those nations,
As He fights in the day of battle.

Judged for persecutioning Israel
Isaiah 63:1-5 (NKJV) Who is this who comes from Edom, With dyed garments from Bozrah,
This One who is glorious in His apparel,
Traveling in the greatness of His strength?--
"I who speak in righteousness, mighty to save."
Why is Your apparel red,
And Your garments like one who treads in the winepress?
"I have trodden the winepress alone

To cause Israel to flee into the wilderness of Edom and Moab and to be so persecuted by the nations that Israel will have to turn to God for help.
Isaiah 16:1 – 5; Ezekiel 20:33 – 35; Daniel 11:40 – 12:7; Hosea 2:14 – 17; Matthew 24:15 – 31; revelations 12

WHY THE RAPTURE?

TO CONCLUDE THE SEVENTIETH WEEK

THE SEVENTIETH WEEK IS THE TRIBULATION

Dan 12:6-7 (NKJV) Then I heard the man clothed in linen, who was above the waters of the river, when he held up his right hand and his left hand to heaven, and swore by Him who lives forever, that it shall be for a time, times, and half a time; and when the power of the holy people has been completely shattered, all these things shall be finished.

GREATLY BELOVED

Dan 9:23-27 At the beginning of thy supplications the commandment came forth, and I am come to shew *thee*; for thou *art* greatly beloved: therefore understand the matter, and consider the vision<u>. **Seventy weeks are determined upon thy people and upon thy holy city, to finish the transgression, and to make an end of sins, and to make reconciliation for iniquity, and to bring in everlasting righteousness,**</u> and to seal up the vision and prophecy, and to anoint the most Holy. Know therefore and understand, *that* from the going forth of the commandment to restore and to build Jerusalem unto the Messiah the Prince *shall be* seven weeks, and threescore and two weeks: the street shall be built again, and the wall, even in troublous times. And after threescore and two weeks shall Messiah be cut off, but not for himself: and the people of the prince that shall come shall destroy the city and the sanctuary; and the end thereof *shall be* with a flood, and unto the end of the war desolations are determined. <u>**And he shall confirm the covenant with many for one week: and in the midst of the week he shall cause the sacrifice and the oblation to cease,**</u> and for the overspreading of abominations he shall make *it* desolate, even until the consummation, and that determined shall be poured upon the desolate.

As you see in the above passage of scripture Dan 9:23-27; there was fulfilled only 69 of the 70 years of captivity and God's wrath on Israel has to be complete according to the Prophet Jeremiah. Israel's captivity or the time of Jacob's trouble must be completed. You as Christians do not have to go through this time of tribulation unless you want to. God has given you a way of escape. ***That way of escape is your salvation.***

WHY THE RAPTURE?

The character of the tribulation
God will pour out his wrath upon all mankind for the wickedness and corruption that even exceeded that of the days of Noah and Lot. They will

reject the truth of God and he will turn them over to strong delusions of the antichrist who will cause them to believe a lie and be damned.

HELL BOUND

Rev 9:19-21 (NKJV) But the rest of mankind, who were not killed by these plagues, did not repent of the works of their hands, that they should not worship demons, and idols of gold, silver, brass, stone, and wood, which can neither see nor hear nor walk. And they did not repent of their murders or their sorceries or their sexual immorality or their thefts.

WHY THE RAPTURE?

DON'T NEGLECT THIS OPPORTUNITY

Heb 2:3-4 (KJV) <u>How shall we escape, if we neglect so great salvation;</u> The question is how shall we escape, if we neglect so great a salvation? We know that when we speak of salvation we cannot help but speak of the salvation that Jesus acquired for our spirit when he conquered spiritual death, and sins, and our sin nature, but this is speaking of salvation of the whole man and of our escape from what is about to come on the earth. The question again is how shall we escape if we neglect the opportunity that has been given to us? <u>**Answer: There is no escape if we neglect this salvation**</u>

KEEP YOUR GARMENT

Rev 16:15
Don't walk in nakedness and shame. If you are part of this body of believers keep your garment, fellowship with the father daily, Watch and pray so that you may escape what is coming.

KNOW THAT YOU CAN ESCAPE

Luke 21:36
We can escape these things that are coming upon the whole earth. The Lord shows us how to escape if we are willing. He says watch therefore and pray always, that you may be found worthy to escape these things that shall come to pass. Do you want to escape?

God wants you to repent

2 Peter 3:1-9
Peter says I'm writing to you to remind you to stir up your pure minds that you may be mindful of the words spoken by the prophets, and of the commandments of us, the apostles of the Lord and Savior knowing this first that scoffers will come in the last days, walking according to their own lust, and saying where is the promise of his coming? They will tell you that since the fathers fell asleep all things continue as they were from the beginning of creation. For this they willfully forget that by the word of God the heavens were of old and the earth standing out of water, and in the water, by which the world that then existed perished, being flooded with water, but the heavens and earth which are now preserved by the same word, are reserved for fire until the day of judgment and perdition of ungodly men. Do not forget this one thing that with the Lord one day is as 1000 years and 1000 years as one day. The Lord is not slack concerning his promises, as some count slackness, but is long-suffering towards us not willing that any should perish but that all should come to repentance.

DO YOU NEED PRAYER?

Are you going through relationship problems?
Are you depressed?
Do you need healing?

Are you unsure of your salvation?
Are you unsure if there's a heaven or hell?
Are you fearing the tribulation?

Let me pray with you a prayer that is guaranteed for God to hear you.

PLEASE PRAY THIS PRAYER FROM YOUR HEART

Dear heavenly father I come before you a sinner.

I believe you sent your son to the earth to live for me, and to die for me, and to be raised from the dead for me, so that I can experience eternal life, and not hell. Thank you for bearing my sins, so that I don't have to. Come into my heart, and live through me, so that I may live for you. Thank you Lord for saving me.

If you prayed this prayer in faith, please direct correspondence to:

HEAVEN BOUND MINISTRIES
James H. Rayner
PO Box #235
6425 LEORNARDTOWN RD
BRYANTOWN, MD. 20617

Reflection

HOW

HOW WILL THE RAPTURE OCCUR?

To see how the rapture is to occur we must first see the indicators. What the Scripture reveals before the rapture is to take place. We must watch the signs. We must also pay attention to the order in which they happen. I am not trying to undermine the authority of God the father, but to give the children of light, more insight so that they may properly prepare, and also to encourage them, while they hope for the Blessed Hope. The word of God says that even though we may not know the time as Christians, but we know the season. Even though Jesus comes as a thief in the night,

RAPTURE READY THE SAINTS

But ye, brethren, are not in darkness, that that day should overtake you as a thief. 1 Thess 5:4-5 says; **Ye are all the children of light.**

HOW WILL THE RAPTURE TAKE PLACE?

The same way the Bible says it is to take place.

1. *To see how the rapture is to take place we must first look at all of what is to happen just before the rapture.*

I BELEIVE IN A RAPTURE BEFORE TRIBULATION

WHY?

WE MUST WATCH AND PRAY

REASON ONE: I believe as it says in Luke 21:36 we must watch, and pray, that we be found worthy to escape all these things that shall come to pass, and to stand before the Son of man.

THE TRIBULATION IS DANGER

REASON TWO: The definition of the word rapture means to snatch out of the way of danger.

GOD KNOWS HOW TO DELIVER

REASON THREE: 2 Pet 2:9 **says: The Lord knoweth how to deliver the godly out of temptations, and to reserve the unjust unto the day of judgment to be punished:**

THE LORD IS OUR SAVIOUR

REASON FOUR: Heb 7:25 says: he is able also to save them to the uttermost that comes unto God by him, seeing he ever liveth to make intercession for them.

HE SAVED NOAH BEFORE THE FLOOD

REASON FIVE: Luke 17:26-27 SAYS: And as it was in the days of Noe, so shall it be also in the days of the Son of man. They did eat, they drank, they married wives, they were given in marriage, until the day that Noe entered into the ark, and the flood came, and destroyed them all.

HE SAVED LOT BEFORE THE FIRE FELL

REASON SIX: Luke 17:28-29 SAYS; Likewise also as it was in the days of Lot; they did eat, they drank, they bought, they sold, they planted, they builded; But the same day that Lot went out of Sodom it rained fire and brimstone from heaven, and destroyed *them* all.

ALL BECAUSE OF JACOB

REASON SEVEN: The tribulation is called the time of Jacobs's trouble. Jacob's name was changed to Israel.

THIS WRATH IS NOT FOR US

REASON EIGHT: 1 Thess 5:9 Says: For God hath not appointed us to wrath, but to obtain salvation by our Lord Jesus Christ,

2. *And then we must see what the Bible says about how the rapture is to take place.*

Matt 24:35-44 For as in the days that were before the flood they were eating and drinking, marrying and giving in marriage, until the day that Noe entered into the ark, And knew not until the flood came, and took them all away; so shall also the coming of the Son of man be.

Notice in the 35<u>th</u> verse, and this verse says that this is before the flood, and they were eating and drinking and marrying and giving in marriage until the day that Noah entered the Ark.
That means that people will be drinking, marrying, and giving in marriage, and other words planning their lives until the rapture happens. Notice the things of the tribulation were not expressed, but the same things that were being done in the day of Noah and no one was aware of salvation until Noah entered the Ark. I believe this is how the rapture is to take place. I believe that we are to enter the Ark in the sky before the flood of tribulation happens.

JEWISH CUSTOM

In Matthew 25 notice: all of the virgins were asleep, five foolish and five wise were all asleep. What determined their going with the bridegroom? ANSWER:

Having enough oil to find their way, and trimming the wick which is actually adorning ones self. I say once again, you cannot go to this wedding in your gym clothes. You must be dressed. Jesus gave his life for your wedding garment, that you may be adorned with a robe of righteousness. **Put it on**

As a thief in the night

Matthew 24:32 says that Jesus will return like a thief in the night. You will not be able to detect his return unless you are what he returns for.

THE RAPTURE

WE MUST UNDERSTAND THAT THE RAPTURE CANNOT OCCUR UNLESS JESUS RETURNS FOR HIS BRIDE. SO HIS RETURN BEGINS THE RAPTURE…AND IT'S ALL ABOUT HIS SON'S WEDDING.

CAUGHT UP

SO WE SHALL BE CAUGHT UP TO MEET JESUS IN THE AIR WHEN HE RETURNS.

Look at the word of GOD

NOTE: *To see how the rapture is to occur we must first see what is recorded to happen just before the rapture.*

Of course the catching away is also performed while our mortal bodies are transformed into glorious bodies, but we must look at all of the other things that happen before the rapture to understand how it is to take place.

Let's start with when we are changed in a twinkling.

OUR BODIES WILL BE CHANGED

1 Cor 15:51-57

Surely the dead in Christ shall rise, but all who rise shall not be dead. The Scriptures say we shall not all sleep for we shall be changed, in a moment in the twinkling of an eye and at the last Trump for the trumpet shall sound and the dead in Christ shall rise incorruptible. We shall be changed. The word says the corruptible must put on incorruption, and the mortal must put on immortality. So when this corruptible shall have put on incorruption, and this mortal shall have put on immortality, and then shall be brought to pass the saying that is written, death is swallowed up in victory. O death where is thy sting? O grave where is thy victory?

We shall not all sleep,

We shall not all die

We shall be changed

So when this corruptible shall have put on incorruption,

and mortal shall have put on immortality

but we shall all be changed, 52 In a moment, in the twinkling of an eye,

Our bodies shall be glorified

in the twinkling = a twinkling is 1/100 of a second

We shall instantly be like him. (Jesus)

1 John 3:1-3 (KJV) Beloved, now are we the sons of God, *and it doth not yet appear what we shall be: but we know that, when he shall appear, we shall be like him;* for we shall see him as he is. 3 And every man that hath this hope in him purifieth himself, even as he is pure.

We shall instantly be like him. (Jesus)

OUR BODIES SHALL BE GLORIFIED, which means that instead of mans glory we shall have the pleasing glory of God, which contains the characteristics of God including the eternal. I am quite sure it is impossible to explain the heavenly to one who has always known the earthly. It is enough just to say we will be like him, because he is heavenly. Jesus has a heavenly body and so shall we.

GODS GLORY IS ETERNAL

Our glory is like a flower that withers

1 Peter 1:24-25

All flesh is like grass here today gone tomorrow and all yet you accomplish and fame fortune and glory in the earth is just like a flower a delicate flower that fades in glory, but the word of God endures for ever.

GLORIFY ME WITH YOURSELF

John 17:5 (KJV) And now, O Father, glorify thou me with thine own self with the glory which I had with thee before the world was.

We will have glorified bodies

1 John 3:2-3 Beloved, now are we the sons of God, and it doth not yet appear what we shall be: but we know that, when he shall appear, we shall be like him; for we shall see him as he is. 3 And every man that hath this hope in him purifieth himself, even as he is pure.

THE BRANCH IS TENDER

Matt 24:32-42 (KJV) Now learn a parable of the fig tree; When his branch is yet tender, and putteth forth leaves, ye know that summer is nigh: 33 So likewise ye, when ye shall see all these things, know that it is near, even at the doors.

The fig tree is Israel. The fig leaves are a sign of life.

THIS GENERATION SHALL NOT PASS UNTIL

34 Verily I say unto you, this generation shall not pass, till all these things be fulfilled. 35 Heaven and earth shall pass away, but my words shall not pass away. 36 but of that day and hour knoweth no man, no, not the angels of heaven, but my Father only.

<u>*This generation is speaking of when Israel became a nation in 1945*</u>
WE ARE STILL OF THAT GENERATION

JUST LIKE THE DAYS OF NOAH

Matt 24:37
We cannot fully understand how the rapture is to take place unless we look at Noah. We see a man told by God to prepare for tribulation which is to come upon the earth. Everyone scoffed ridiculed and persecuted Noah because of his insane words. It had never rained before, the miss went up from the ground, but the rain did not fall up into his point, however this man Noah believed God, and when he was finished the Ark and all of what God had told him to do he entered in and the door was shut. The word of God says that the flood came and took all of the people away; so shall be the coming of the Son of Man.

OUR JOB IS TO WATCH

Then shall two be in the field; the one shall be taken, and the other left. Two women shall be grinding at the mill; the one shall be taken, and the other left. Watch therefore: for ye know not what hour your Lord doth come.

WE SUFFER RIDICULE AND REJECTION

Luke 17:25-26 *But first must he suffer many things, and be rejected of this generation. And as it was in the days of Noe, so shall it be also in the days of the Son of man.*

<u>BLESSED IS THAT SERVANT WHOM THE LORD FIND DOING</u>

Matt 24:45-51 (KJV) Who then is a faithful and wise servant, whom his lord hath made ruler over his household, to give them meat in due season? 46 Blessed is that servant, whom his lord when he cometh shall find so doing. 47 Verily I say unto you, that he shall make him ruler over all his goods. 48 But and if that evil servant shall say in his heart, My lord delayeth his coming; 49 And shall begin to smite his fellow servants, and to eat and drink with the drunken; 50 The lord of that servant shall come in a day when he looketh not for him, and in an hour that he is not aware of, 51 And shall cut him asunder, and appoint him his portion with the hypocrites: there shall be weeping and gnashing of teeth.

But and if that evil servant shall say in his heart, My lord delayeth his coming; And shall begin to smite his fellow servants, and to eat and drink with the drunken;

<u>The lord of that servant shall come in a day when he looketh not for him, and in an hour that he is not aware of,</u>

And shall cut him asunder, and appoint him his portion with the hypocrites: there shall be weeping and gnashing of teeth.

The hypocrites shall be left and so shall the unfaithful servant. He shall have his place in the earth during the tribulation where there is weeping and gnashing of teeth. Jesus is coming for the faithful servant, not be unfaithful.

This parable shows that waiting on Jesus, and for the rapture is to be a lifestyle. Because you are sanctified and washed and are no longer a part of the world but you are children of the light who should be walking in the light, we need to make walking in the spirit a lifestyle we have got to become rapture ready. If we live in the sanctified life as a lifestyle we would not have to worry about who's going in rapture, because if we walk in the spirit we shall not fulfill the lust of the flesh.

WE MUST UNDERSTAND THAT THE RAPTURE CANNOT OCCUR UNTIL JESUS RETURNS FOR HIS BRIDE. SO HIS RETURN BEGINS THE RAPTURE…AND IT'S ALL ABOUT HIS WEDDING.

SO WE SHALL BE CAUGHT UP TO MEET JESUS IN THE AIR WHEN HE RETURNS.

LOOK AT WHAT HAPPENS BEFORE THE RAPTURE

LOOK AT THE SEASON; look at the word of GOD

NOTE: To see how the rapture is to occur we must first see what is recorded to happen before the rapture, in the word of God.

FIRST THERE MUST BE A FALLING AWAY

This falling away may occur because many Christians have given up. They have listened to the airwaves that say that God is not real. They have listened to the airways that say religion is not real, but we believe in a God that exist outside of the word of God. There are many groups that say that Jesus does not exist. We also have scoffers and mockers who ask where is Jesus and when is he to come, because everything goes on just the way it always has. We have another group that says that God has no son, but yet they say Jesus as a prophet.

Then there are those who know the truth and the only reason they know the truth is because they have received Jesus Christ into their heart and he has become a part of them. It's too late to tell them that Jesus don't exist, because they walked with him every day. These are those who are zealous of good works, and are ready to go back with Jesus when he comes.

*The not so serious saints will leave the church

Christians are leaving the church at a rate of 300,000 a year.
As of 2014 Islam is growing faster in the US than Christianity.
Pastors are leaving the ministry at the rate of 15000 per year.

*And then that man of sin is to be revealed.

FALLING AWAY

2 Thess 2:1-4 (NKJV) *Now, brethren, concerning the coming of our Lord Jesus Christ and our gathering together to Him, we ask you, 2 not to be soon shaken in mind or troubled, either by spirit or by word or by letter, as if from us, as though the day of Christ had come. 3 Let no one deceive you by any means; **for that Day will not come unless the falling away comes first, and the man of sin is revealed,** the son of perdition, 4 who opposes and exalts himself above all that is called God or that is worshipped, so that he sits as God.*

2 Tim 3:1-13 (KJV) *this knows also, that in the last day's perilous times shall come. 2 For men shall be lovers of their own selves, covetous, boasters, proud, blasphemers, disobedient to parents, unthankful, unholy, 3 Without* *natural affection, trucebreakers, false accusers, incontinent, fierce, despisers of those that are good, 4 Traitors, heady, high-minded, lovers of pleasures more than lovers of God;*

INIQUITY SHALL ABOUND

Matt 24:8-14

All these are the beginning of sorrows. Then shall they deliver you up to be afflicted, and shall kill you: and ye shall be hated of all nations for my name's sake.

And then shall many be offended, and shall betray one another, and shall hate one another.

And many false prophets shall rise, and shall deceive many.

And because iniquity shall abound, the love of many shall wax cold.

But he that shall endure unto the end, the same shall be saved.

*And this gospel of the kingdom shall be preached in all the world for a witness unto all nations;
and then shall the end come.*

THE MYSTERY OF INIQUITY

Statues of Satan in the US

*NOTICE: STATUES OF SATAN WERE NOT PROPOSED TO BE ERECTED IN ARIZONA AND OKLAHOMA UNTIL **SOMEONE SAID:** THE UNITED STATES IS NO LONGER A CHRISTIAN NATION.*

Don't you believe it. The devil must unravel what God has done to make this no longer a great nation, a Christian nation. Regardless of all the evil that has taken place in this country God has formatted the Constitution with godly in biblical principals and it must be destroyed for this nation to be destroyed.

SATANIC WORSHIP IN THE US

THIS DOOR WAS OPENED BY WORDS

Prov 18:21 (NKJV) *Death and life are in the power of the tongue, And those who love it will eat its fruit.*

*WE HAVE OPPOSITION EVEN DISPLAYING THE TEN COMMANDMENTS NOW. EVEN THOUGH WE ARE A NATION FOUNDED ON JUDEO-CHRISTIAN GODLY PRINCIPLES.

We have already seen iniquity abound in this nation, and we have seen the abomination of homosexuality given a lawful place in this nation. Throughout all of civilization this has always been the nation crusher.

People are looked at with disdain when they speak the name of Jesus in the United States, where our nation was founded on godly principles.

THERE WILL BE A STRONG DELUSION
FOR THOSE WHO WOULD RATHER BELIEVE A LIE

*The excepted religion of the day is the religion that hates Christianity and the crucified Christ. It is organized religion that hates and opposes Christians. The Bible is very clear that in the last days **there would be a great falling away from the true gospel.** Jesus says many shall come in my name saying I am Christ and **shall deceive many,** and because iniquity shall abound **the love of many shall wax cold and there shall arise false Christs, and false prophets,** and shall show great signs and* *wonders insomuch that if it were possible they should deceive even the very elect. The Word of God also says that* **the man of sin shall be revealed in his coming after the workings of Satan with all power and signs and lying wonders** *and with all deceivableness of unrighteousness in them that perish because they received not the love of the truth that they might be saved.* **And for this cause God shall send them a strong delusion, that they should believe a lie; that they all might be damned who believed not the truth but had pleasure in unrighteousness.** *There is to be a strong delusion. Maybe it's the fulfillment of people having seen flying saucers all of these years.*

What if that was a setup, and the buying of time to get certain demons into the earth to cause this strong delusion?

What if that was a setup and buying of time to get certain technology created? Holographic technology.

Maybe the nephilim (Fallen Angels), are to return.

* Christians have become public enemy number one in the US. Our rapture may possibly be explained as an abduction by the aliens to take away the heretics, or fanatical christians. Who of us will be here to dispute it after the rapture?

Maybe there is to be a staged UFO landing telling us to worship them.

A STRONG DELUSION

2 Thess 2:10-11 (NKJV) and with all unrighteous deception among those who perish, because <u>they did not receive the love of the truth, that they might be saved. And for this reason God will send them a</u> **strong delusion,** that they should believe the lie,

We include the strong delusion and the great deception because it will probably begin before the rapture. As I have stated before, in order to see how the rapture is to occur we must know what is to happen before the rapture.

because they did not receive the love of the truth, that they might be saved.

And for this reason God will send them strong delusion, that they should believe the lie,

And for what reason?

because they did not receive the love of the truth, that they might be saved.

<u>They did not receive the word of God.</u>

WATCH OUT FOR THE GREAT DECEPTION

This may take place after the rapture and if it were possible would fool even the elect; and may be used to explain the disappearance of so many people, to the masses. The elect must be referring to the tribulation saints. **(Those who will die during the tribulation).**

STAGED DECEPTION

THIS SCENERIO WILL NOT BE TRUE. YOU MUST WATCH AND PRAY

Fallen Angels, or the nephilim may be here to prove to the agnostics, atheists, and backsliders that we are the offspring of aliens. What if that is the strong delusion? What if you are being deceived by demons. Satan is a deceiver and the greatest liar that ever lived. Don't wait until you get to hell for Satan to laugh at you and admit it.

<u>*The false Christ is lying, just by being here.*</u>

He comes the wrong way

*This also explains how the rapture is to take place. There are many false prophets, and false Christ's walking the streets today, but the word of God makes it clear that Christ will return the same way he went up into the clouds. This in itself will let you know that Christ is not walking the streets in physical form. The false Christ's that you admire, and serve, and pray to, is not he.

DON'T BE DECEIVED

JESUS IS COMING IN THE CLOUDS

HE WILL NOT WALK DOWN THE STREETS OF OKLAHOMA

HE WILL NOT BE IN THE DESERT

HE WILL NOT BE IN SOME ROOM

JESUS WILL NOT RETURN ANY OTHER WAY

Matt 24:23-27
There will be people who will be telling you where to go to find Christ in the earth. There's no reason to go Jesus has already said he's coming the same way he left. The Angels told the disciples the same way that you see Jesus leaving is a way he will return in the clouds. Stop believing every body. Stop believing these false prophets if they tell you he's over there, don't even go to look for him because it goes against what he has originally said.

LISTEN TO WHAT THE ANGELS SAID

Acts 1:10-11 (NKJV) And while they looked steadfastly toward heaven as He went up, behold, two men stood by them in white apparel, 11 who also said, "Men of Galilee, why do you stand gazing up into heaven? **This same Jesus, who was taken up from you into heaven, will so come in like manner as you saw Him go into heaven.**

JESUS WILL RETURN THE SAME WAY/ THROUGH THE CLOUDS

Acts 1:8-9 (KJV) And when he had spoken these things, while they beheld, he was taken up; and a cloud received him out of their sight.

Will so come in like manner as you saw him go

*The Angels made it very clear, that the Jesus that the disciples knew is the Jesus they saw go into heaven. The Jesus of the Bible. There is no excuse for anyone who knows the word of God to follow after a false Jesus. If you know Jesus and have an intimate relationship with him, how can you be deceived? Anyone who proclaims to be Jesus and is walking on the earth is not Jesus because he did not return as Jesus said that he would. He did not return as the Angels proclaimed to the disciples.

THAT MEANS UP, NOT OVER THERE

JESUS WILL COME AS LIGHTNING FLASHES FROM THE EAST

HE'S NOT IN THE DESERT, OR THE INNER ROOMS

Matt 24:23-27 (NKJV) Then if anyone says to you, 'Look, here is the Christ!' or 'There!' **do not believe it.** 24 For false christs and false prophets will rise and show great signs and wonders to deceive, if possible, even the elect. 25 See, I have told you beforehand. <u>26</u>

Therefore if they say to you, 'Look, He is in the desert!' do not go out; or 'Look, He is in the inner rooms!' do not believe it. **27 For as the lightning comes from the east and flashes to the west, so also will the coming of the Son of Man be.**

HOW HE IS TO RETURN TO EARTH

We are not to believe anyone who tells us that Jesus is over here or Jesus is over there. You have got to know for yourself that the word of God is true and that he has made it so, and that you should know how he is to return.

ACTIVATE YOUR FAITH

SURE THERE ARE SCOFFERS
SURE THERE ARE COMPLAINERS
SURE THERE ARE MOCKERS
SURE THERE ARE THOSE WHO CAUSE DIVISION
THAT IS WHY WE WERE GIVEN A MEASURE OF FAITH
THAT IS ALSO WHY WE HAVE GODS WORD

IF THERE WAS NO OPPPOSITION, WE WOULDN'T NEED FAITH.

Faith cometh by hearing and hearing by the word of God. **Get into the word of God and increase your faith.**

WALKING AFTER THEIR OWN LUSTS

2 Peter 3:3-4 (KJV) Knowing this first, that there shall come in the last days scoffers, **walking after their own lusts,** 4 And saying, Where is the promise of his coming? for since the fathers fell asleep, all things continue as they were from the beginning of the creation.

SCOFFERS DESIRE TO BE ADMIRED

Jude 1:15-16 (KJV) To execute judgment upon all, and to convince all that are ungodly among them of all their ungodly deeds which they have ungodly committed, and of all their hard speeches which ungodly sinners have spoken against him. These are murmurers, complainers, walking after their own lusts; and their mouth speaketh great swelling words, **having men's persons in admiration because of advantage**

THEY DON'T HAVE THE SPIRIT

Jude 1:19
They separate themselves from those who actually have the Spirit and because of their character and the lusts of their hearts they cannot agree with those who have the Spirit, so they must separate. Can two walk together unless they agree?

HOW DID WE GET TO THIS POINT?

This is the day when the perilous times mentioned in *2 Tim 3:1-5* has come. **To put it in simpler terms dangerous times.** Men are now lovers of their own selves. Just look at the ministers on the forefront TV evangelists, using God to make wealth for their own personal gain, when the Scripture says in Mat 16:24 that if you desire to come after me, deny yourself, pick up your cross and follow me. Look at the rich young ruler who asked Jesus what more does he need to do to inherit eternal life. Jesus told him to;

Sell what you have and give to the poor, and you will have treasure in heaven; and come, follow Me." Matt 19:21

The rich young ruler walked away with his head down because he couldn't give it up. The word of God says that they will be lovers of their own selves, covetous, boasters, proud, blasphemers, disobedient to parents, unthankful, unholy, without natural affection, trucebreakers, false accusers, incontinent, fierce, despisers of those that are good, traitors, heady, high-minded, lovers of pleasures more than lovers of God; having a form of godliness, but denying the power thereof: from such turn away. I am convinced that this was a key element in developing scoffers, mockers, grumblers, complainers etc. None of these have the spirit. All of these are walking after their own lust.

We are truly living in the last day

CHRIST THE FIRST FRUITS

1 Cor 15:20 (NKJV) But now Christ is risen from the dead, and has become the first fruits of those who have fallen asleep.

JESUS CAME FIRST THAT WE MAY GO WITH HIM

CHRIST'S AT HIS COMING

1 Cor 15:22-24 (NKJV) But each one in his own order: **Christ the first fruits, afterward those who are Christ's at His coming.** 24 Then comes the end, when He delivers the kingdom to God the Father, when He puts an end to all rule and all authority and power.

JESUS OUR FIRST FRUITS

The first fruits were waved before the father, by the priest. Once the first fruits were waved in the Temple there was then a sacrifice proclaiming the whole field sanctified and holy. Jesus is our first fruits. **Jesus made the whole field sanctified and holy. It is he who sanctifies us.**

MANY WILL BE DECEIVED

Matt 24:5-14 (NKJV) for many will come in my name, saying, 'I am the Christ,' and will deceive many.

*The only reason they are deceived is because either they didn't read the word of God, or they don't believe the word of God or they don't want God, and **because of this they are in error.***

E. Error - 1) plane - to go astray from the set path, or order of things. Jas 5:19; 1 Jn 4:6 Error

Error - 2) astocheo - to disreguard, or ignore that which is right. 1 Tim 6:21; 2 Tim 2:18

HOW DO YOU TELL A WOLF?

Matt 7:15-18 (NKJV) "Beware of false prophets, who come to you in sheep's clothing, but inwardly they are ravenous wolves. **16 You will know them by their fruits.** Do men gather grapes from thorn bushes or figs from thistles? 17 Even so, every good tree bears good fruit, but a bad tree bears bad fruit. 18 A good tree cannot bear bad fruit, nor can a bad tree bear good fruit.

REMEMBER GOD IS GOOD; THE DEVIL IS BAD

YOU MUST LEARN TO BE A FRUIT INSPECTOR

Do men gather grapes from thorn bushes or figs from thistles?

DONT EVEN TRY TO GET GRAPES FROM THORNBUSHES
DON'T EVEN TRY TO GET FIGS FROM THISTLES

THORNBUSH = A BUSH OF THORNS THAT PRODUCE THORNS THAT

CAUSE SHARP PAIN, IRRITATION AND DISCOMFORT-+

THISTLE = MAY HAVE A FLOWER SUCH AS A DAISY, BUT TYPICALLY HAS A PRICKLY STEM.

IS YOUR SPIRIT UNCOMFORTABLE?

... Does that banana have bruises on it?

Does that Apple have worms in it?

IT IS NOT GOOD FRUIT!

Does it line up with the words of God?

Compare the character to JESUS / YESHUA

1 Tim 6:1-5 (KJV) Let as many servants as are under the yoke count their own masters worthy of all honour, that the name of God and his doctrine be not blasphemed. 2 And they that have believing masters, let them not despise them, because they are brethren; but rather do them service, because they are faithful and beloved, partakers of the benefit. These things teach and exhort. 3 If any man teach otherwise, and consent not to wholesome words, even the words of our Lord Jesus Christ, and to the doctrine which is according to godliness; 4 He is proud, knowing nothing, but doting about questions and strifes of words, whereof cometh envy, strife, railings, evil surmisings, 5 Perverse disputings of men of corrupt minds, and destitute of the truth, supposing that gain is godliness: **from such withdraw thyself.**

KEEP THE FAITH

2 Tim 2:15-18 (KJV) Study to shew thyself approved unto God, a workman that needeth not to be ashamed, **rightly dividing the word of truth.** 16 But shun profane and vain babblings: for they will increase unto more ungodliness. 17 And their word will eat as doth a canker: of whom are Hymenaeus and Philetus; 18 who concerning the truth have erred, **saying that the resurrection is past already;** and overthrow the faith of some.

TEACH NO OTHER GOSPEL

Gal 1:8-9 (KJV) but though we, **or an angel from heaven, preach any other gospel unto you than that, which we have preached unto you,** let him be accursed. 9 As we said before, so say I now again, **If any man preach any other gospel unto you than that ye have received,** let him be accursed.

The word of God is so important that we cannot afford to abuse it, miss use it, change it, take away from it, or add to it.

Rev 22:18-19 (NKJV) For I testify to everyone who hears the words of the prophecy of this book: If anyone adds to these things, God will add to him the plagues that are written in this book; [19] and if anyone takes away from the words of the book of this prophecy, God shall take away his part from the Book of Life, from the holy city, and *from* the things which are written in this book.

We cannot add to the word of God. I noticed many religions at another book while studying the Bible. I'm not talking about commentaries or the sources or books that help you to understand the true word of God, but a whole new added Revelation from another prophet other than the Lord and Savior Jesus Christ. The word of God says that if anyone adds to these things, God will add to him the plagues that are written in this book. And then there are other religions that don't believe the whole word of God therefore they take out what is appropriate for their religion. The word of God says if anyone takes away from the words of the book of this prophecy, God shall take away his part from the book of life, from the holy city, and from the things which are written in this book.

JESUS SAID, COME AND DRINK IF YOU THIRST

John 7:37-39 (NKJV) on the last day, that great day of the feast, Jesus stood and cried out, saying, "If anyone thirsts, let him come to me and drink. 38 He who believes in me, as the Scripture has said, **out of his heart will Flow Rivers of living water."** 39 But this He spoke concerning the Spirit, whom those believing in Him would receive; for the Holy Spirit was not yet given, because Jesus was not yet glorified.

The man of God should not be as a Wolf in sheep's clothing coming to shear the sheep. The man of God should be used by God if anyone thirst he should be able to go to the man of God and drink. The man of God should always point to Jesus and not to himself as if he is some great one. The true man of God can tell you how to quench your thirst through God.

38 He who believes in me, as the Scripture has said, out of his heart will Flow Rivers of living water."

NEVER THIRST AGAIN

John 4:13-14 (NKJV) "Whoever drinks of this water will thirst again, **14 but whoever drinks of the water that I shall give him will never thirst.** But the water that I shall give him will become in him a fountain of water springing up into everlasting life."

The man of God should be able to reveal the thirsts quencher to the thirsty, and enable them to never thirst again for the world or the things in the world.

CLOUDS WITHOUT WATER

Jude 1:12 (NKJV) these are spots in your love feasts, while they feast with you without fear, **serving only themselves. They are clouds without water, carried about by the winds;** late autumn trees without fruit, twice dead, pulled up by the roots.

The man of God should not be a cloud without water. A cloud without water looks like it's ready to rain and the cool things down and the quench the thirst of the people and to make them satisfied and yet they just look like a cloud, for there is no water. Looking like autumn trees without fruit.

Jesus cursed the fig tree because it looked like it had fruit, there were signs of life in the fact that it had leaves, but when he got near he saw that there were leaves only and no fruit.

Make sure the man of God is a; what you see you get pastor.

They corrupt themselves

Jude 1:10-11 (KJV) but these speak evil of those things which they know not: but what they know naturally, as brute beasts, in those things they corrupt themselves. 11 Woe unto them! For they have gone in the way of Cain, and ran greedily after the error of Balaam for reward, and perished in the gainsaying of Core.

It is important that the prophet is not there for profit. But to profit the Lord, and the body of Christ. It's nice to pay a pastor it's nice that he has a salary, but the word of God says that if anyone wishes to follow me, let him deny himself, pick up his cross, and follow me.

AVOID BAD DOCTRINE

Romans 16:17-18
Watch out for those who do not serve our Lord Jesus Christ. You should be able to tell because they are too busy serving themselves. And of course they will cause division and offenses contrary to the doctrine that Jesus taught.

*IT IS CRUCIAL TO GET A GOOD PASTOR. ONE WHO TEACHES THE WHOLE TRUTH, NOT JUST MONEY; ONE WHO IS MORE CONCERNED **ABOUT YOUR SOUL AND ETERNITY AND NOT JUST, YOU HAVING YOUR BEST LIFE NOW, OR LEARNING TO MAKE MONEY, OR BUILDING YOUR KINGDOM IN THE EARTH.***

He should be one who desires to see your soul prosper.

SUFFERING CAN'T BE COMPARED

Romans 8:18 (NKJV) *For I consider that the sufferings of this present time are not worthy to be compared with the glory which shall be revealed in us.*

*YOU CANNOT COMPARE THIS LIFE WITH FUTURE GLORY NO TIME TO COLLECT TOYS; **IT IS TIME TO OBEY GOD.** QUESTION: HOW ARE WE GOING TO ESCAPE? ANSWER: **BY OBEYING GOD!***

HOW SHALL WE ESCAPE?

Heb 2:3 (NKJV) *how shall we escape if we neglect so great a salvation, which at the first began to be spoken by the Lord, and was confirmed to us by those who heard Him,*

Rev 3:10 because you have kept my command to persevere, I also will keep you from the hour of trial which shall come upon the whole world, to test those who dwell on the earth.

THIS IS HOW WE ESCAPE

This is the church of Philadelphia that the command of the Lord. Because they kept the command with perseverance God will now keep them from the hour of trial which shall come upon the whole earth. This is how we escape.

MANY AFFLICTIONS IF YOU ARE RIGHTEOUS

The Lord didn't say it would be easy
Psalms 34:19 (NKJV) *Many are the afflictions of the righteous, But the Lord delivers him out of them all.*

HOW TO MAKE IT IN

Matt 16:24-27
Jesus said if anyone desires to come after me let him deny himself and take up his cross and follow me for whoever desires to save his life will lose it but whoever loses his life for my sake will find it. What does it profit a man to gain the whole world and lose his soul, or what will a man give in exchange for his soul? For the Son of Man will come in the glory of his father with his Angels and then he will reward each according to his works.

DENY YOURSELF AND PICK UP YOUR CROSS

"If anyone desires to come after me, let him deny himself, and take up his cross, and follow me.

WHY GAIN THE WHOLE WORLD, WHEN ONE DAY YOU ARE GOING TO DIE?

26 For what profit is it to a man if he gains the whole world, and loses his own soul?

WHAT'S YOUR PRICE, FOR YOUR SOUL?

Many a celebrity has already shown their price for their soul. Many a person in Hollywood and business has shown their price. **WHATS YOURS?**

A private jet?
A Bentley?
A twelve million dollar home.?
A few short moments of fame?
To sleep with someone famous?
To be someone famous?

WHATS YOUR POISON?
FAME, FORTUNE, or FEMALES (FELLAS)
GOLD, GLORY, or GALS. (GUYS)

FACE IT; IT ALWAYS GOES BACK TO:

1 John 2:15-17 (NKJV) For all that is in the world--**the lust of the flesh, the lust of the eyes, and the pride of life**--is not of the Father, but is of the world. 17 And the world is passing away, and the lust of it; but he who does the will of God abides forever.

The lust of the flesh, the lust of the eyes, and the pride of life

EVE

*that it was pleasant to the eyes, - **LUST OF THE EYE***
*and a tree desirable to make one wise, - **PRIDE OF LIFE***
saw that the tree was good for food, - ***LUST OF THE FLESH***

SATAN BRINGS NOTHING NEW

Gen 3:5-8 (NKJV) So when the woman saw that the tree was good for food, that it was pleasant to the eyes, and a tree desirable to make one wise, she took of its fruit and ate. She also gave to her husband with her, and he ate. 7 Then the eyes of both of them were opened, and they knew that they were naked; and they sewed fig leaves together and made themselves coverings. 8 And they heard the sound of the Lord God walking in the garden in the cool of the day, and Adam and his wife hid themselves from the presence of the Lord God among the trees of the garden.

So when the woman saw that the tree was good for food, that it was pleasant to the eyes, and a tree desirable to make one wise, she took of its fruit and ate.

NOT OF THE FATHER / OF THE WORLD

that it was pleasant to the eyes, - ***LUST OF THE EYE***
and a tree desirable to make one wise, - ***PRIDE OF LIFE***
saw that the tree was good for food, - ***LUST OF THE FLESH***

WE ARE CONTENT
1 Tim 6:7-10 (NKJV) And having food and clothing, with these we shall be content. <u>**9 But those who desire to be rich fall into temptation and a snare, and into many foolish and harmful lusts which drown men in destruction and perdition.**</u> 10 For the love of money is a root of all kinds of evil, for which <u>**some have strayed from the faith in their greediness,**</u> and pierced themselves through with many sorrows.

PRINCE AND POWER OF THE AIR (SATAN)

Eph 2:2 (NKJV) in which you once walked according to the course of this world, according to the prince of the power of the air, the spirit who now works in the sons of disobedience

This is the age of deception

COVETING MONEY IS DANGEROUS

But those who desire to be rich fall into temptation and a snare, and into many foolish and harmful lusts which drown men in destruction and perdition.

Many have fallen in love with money, and have fallen in love with a certain lifestyle, which leads to building your kingdom on earth, rather than putting your treasure in heaven.

ERRED FROM THE FAITH

1 Tim 6:10 (KJV) for the love of money is the root of all evil: which while some coveted after, they have erred from the faith, and pierced themselves through with many sorrows.

IT CAUSES YOU TO LEAVE YOUR FIRST LOVE

some have strayed from the faith in their covetousness.

RULES FOR HAVING WEALTH (MONEY)
1 Tim 6:16-21 (NKJV) who alone has immortality, dwelling in unapproachable light, whom no man has seen or can see, to whom be honor and everlasting power. Amen.

17 **Command those** who are rich in this present age not to be haughty, nor to trust in uncertain riches but in the living God, who

gives us richly all things to enjoy. 18 Let them do good, that they be rich in good works, ready to give, willing to share, 19 storing up for themselves a good foundation for the time to come, that they may lay hold on eternal life.

20 O Timothy! Guard what was committed to your trust, avoiding the profane and idle babblings and contradictions of what is falsely called knowledge-- 21 by professing it some have strayed concerning the faith. Grace be with you. Amen.

God does not mind you being rich. He does however mind you being covetous, greedy, lustful, forsaking your calling, falling into error, being distracted by the world, becoming a lover of the world, **having to choose between your kingdom and God's kingdom**.

YOU MUST

Not be haughty
Not trust in uncertain riches but trust in the living God,
Do good
Be rich in good works
Be ready to distribute
Communicate = share or exchange

THESE WILL LAY UP A GOOD FOUNDATION AGAINST THE TIME TO COME, THAT THEY MAY LAY HOLD TO ETERNAL LIFE.

SIGNS OF THESE TIMES

WARS AND RUMORS OF WARS / THE END IS NOT YET

6 And you will hear of wars and rumors of wars. See that you are not troubled; for all these things must come to pass, but the end is not yet.

NATIONS AND KINGDOMS AGAINST EACH OTHER

7 For nation will rise against nation, and kingdom against kingdom. And there will be famines, pestilences, and earthquakes in various places. 8 All these are the beginning of sorrows.

CHRISTIANS DIE AND ARE HATED FOR CHRIST SAKE

9 Then they will deliver you up to tribulation and kill you, and you will be hated by all nations for My name's sake. 10 And then many will be offended, will betray one another, and will hate one another.

MANY FALSE PROPHETS / **REMEMBER HOW CHRIST RETURNS**

11 Then many false prophets will rise up and deceive many.

LAWLESSNESS ABOUNDS

12 And because lawlessness will abound,

WHERE IS THE LOVE?

the love of many will grow cold.

YOU MUST ENDURE TO THE END

13 But he who endures to the end shall be saved.

__Matt 10:22 (NKJV)__ And you will be hated by all for My name's sake. But he who endures to the end will be saved.

THE GOSPEL AS A WITNESS/ **A WITNESS** BECAUSE OF GODS GREAT WORKS THROUGH US

14 And this gospel of the kingdom will be preached in all the world as a witness to all the nations, and then the end will come.

JESUS RETURNS IN THE CLOUDS

1 Thess 4:16-18 (NKJV) For the Lord Himself will descend from heaven with a shout, with the voice of an archangel, and with the trumpet of God. **And the dead in Christ will rise first. 17 Then we who are alive and remain shall be caught up together with them in the clouds to meet the Lord in the air**. And thus we shall always be with the Lord. 18 Therefore comfort one another with these words. **In the clouds** to meet the Lord in the air.

YOUR REDEMPTION DRAWS NEAR
LOOK UP AND LIFT UP YOUR HEADS

Luke 21:25-28 (NKJV)"And there will be signs in the sun, in the moon, and in the stars; and on the earth distress of nations, with perplexity, the sea and the waves roaring; 26 men's hearts failing them from fear and the expectation of those things which are coming on the earth, for the powers of heaven will be shaken. 27 Then they will see the Son of Man coming in a cloud with power and great glory. 28 Now when these things begin to happen, look up and lift up your heads, because your redemption draws near."

WHAT THINGS

signs in the sun, signs in the moon, signs in the stars, distress of nations with perplexity, the sea and the waves roaring, men's hearts failing them from fear, expectation of those things which are coming on the earth, the heavens and the earth shaken

we have seen the blood moons, we have heard of the asteroid headed for the earth, we've heard of Isis murdering Americans, we've heard of the tsunamis and the waves roaring, millionaires

jumping out of windows for fear of what is coming up on the earth, and make no mistake the heavens and the earth shall be shaken. YOUR REDEMPTION IS NEARER THAN BEFORE THESE THINGS OCURRED. AND ALL HAVE ALREADY OCCURRED. January 2016.

AS HE RETURNS

1 John 3:1-3 (NKJV) Behold what manner of love the Father has bestowed on us, that we should be called children of God! Therefore the world does not know us, because it did not know Him. 2 Beloved, now we are children of God; and it has not yet been revealed what we shall be, but we know that when He is revealed, we shall be like Him, for we shall see Him as He is. 3 And **everyone who has this hope in Him purifies himself,** just as He is pure.

So how must the rapture take place?

AFTER THESE THINGS

Luke 21:25-28 (NKJV) "And there will be signs in the sun, in the moon, and in the stars; and on the earth distress of nations, with perplexity, the sea and the waves roaring; 26 men's hearts failing them from fear and the expectation of those things which are coming on the earth, for the powers of heaven will be shaken. 27 Then they will **see the Son of Man coming in a cloud with power and great glory.**

LOOK UP, YOUR REDEMPTION DRAWS NEAR

28 Now when these things begin to happen, look up and lift up your heads, because **your redemption draws near.**"

1 Thess 4:16-18 (KJV) For the Lord himself shall descend from heaven with a shout, with the voice of the archangel, and with the

trump of God: and the dead in Christ shall rise first: 17 Then we which are alive and remain shall be caught up together with them in the clouds, to meet the Lord in the air: and so shall we ever be with the Lord. 18 Wherefore comfort one another with these words.

THE RIGHTEOUS TAKEN OUT OF THE DEAD

Out of the dead - **Ek neckron** means (out of the dead)

To resurrect the dead in Christ from out of the wicked dead

and with the trump of God: and **the dead in Christ shall rise first:** out of the dead

ASSURANCE THAT I MIGHT ATTAIN UNTO THE RESURRECTION FROM THE DEAD

Phil 3:11-12 (KJV) If by any means I might attain unto the resurrection of the dead. 12 Not as though I had already attained, either were already perfect: but I follow after, if that I may apprehend that for which also I am apprehended of Christ Jesus.

1 Cor 15:21 (KJV) For since by man *came* death, by man *came* also the resurrection of the dead.

Ek neckron means (out of the dead)

To resurrect the dead in Christ from out of the wicked dead

The rapture is a bonus. Even if the rapture did not occur, the mere fact that our God is able, and desires to resurrect us from the grave to reward us for the little that we've done in comparison to what Christ has done for us, is more than wonderful and more than enough for us to serve him.

From out of the dead

(resurrection from out of the dead.) leaving the wicked dead

1 Thess 4:15-16 (NKJV) [15] For this we say to you by the word of the Lord, that we who are alive *and* remain until the coming of the Lord will by no means precede those who are asleep. [16] For the Lord Himself will descend from heaven with a shout, with the voice of an archangel, and with the trumpet of God. And the dead in Christ will rise first.

RIGHTEOUS DEAD - RAISED AT HIS COMING
WE WHO ARE ALIVE - ALSO RAISED AT HIS COMING

EK NECKRON - THE RIGHTEOUS DEAD WILL BE RAISED **OUT OF THE DEAD**
THOSE WHO REMAIN ARE THE WICKED DEAD. THEY WILL BE RAISED AND JUDGED IN ANOTHER THOUSAND YEARS

CAUGHT UP

17 Then we which are alive and remain shall be **caught up** together with them in the clouds, to meet the Lord in the air: and so shall we ever be with the Lord.

CAUGHT UP / RAPTURE = HARPAZO
HARPAZO - to be snatched out of <u>the way of harm or danger</u>

THE WAY OF DANGER IS HERE
2 Tim 3:1 (KJV) This know also, that in the last days perilous times shall come.

PERILOUS = DANGEROUS

1 Thess 4:16-17 (KJV) For the Lord himself shall descend from heaven with a shout, with the voice of the archangel, and with the trump of God: and **the dead in Christ** shall rise first: 17 Then we which are alive and remain shall be caught up together with them in the clouds, to meet the Lord in the air: and so shall we ever be with the Lord.

Koimethentas means - they which are asleep
The real way to say; **the dead in Christ**
Koimethentas expresses that the body is asleep,
but the soul is not.

* I PRESENT TO YOU THAT THE SOUL IS IN HEAVEN ONLY TO RETURN WITH CHRIST TO PICK UP THE TRANSFORMED BODY AT THE RAPTURE

ONLY THE FATHER KNOWS WHEN

Matt 24:36-51 (KJV) But of that day and hour knoweth no man, no, not the angels of heaven, but my Father only.

THIS IS HOW THE RAPTURE IS TO HAPPEN

Matt 24:37-39 But as the days of Noe were, so shall also the coming of the Son of man be. 38 For as in the days that were before the flood they were eating and drinking, marrying and giving in marriage, until the day that Noe entered into the ark, 39And knew not until the flood came, and took them all away; so shall also the coming of the Son of man be.

SO SHALL THE COMING OF THE SON OF MAN BE

Notice the days before the flood. People were doing just what they're doing right now; eating and drinking, marrying and giving in marriage, pleasing themselves and not doing as Noah did. Noah was preparing himself and his family for the coming tribulation. Notice the tribulation has not yet taken place. Look at what they were doing. **<u>So shall the coming of the Son of Man be.</u>**

THIS IS OUR MEASURING STICK
AS THE DAYS OF NOAH WERE

The flood is the tribulation, and that is pretty evident because it is what destroyed the people. The flood was also the wrath of God because of evil and perversion in the earth.

The Ark is what saved the family that God ordained to be saved. Those who believed the wrath was coming, and got on board.

Jesus and his returning in the clouds is our Ark of salvation from the destruction and the tribulation that is to come.

Make no mistake we are also working on an ark just as Noah worked on an ark. And when God is ready we must look up, for our redemption draws nigh.

<u>Some are not going; You must be ready to go</u>
Matt 24:40 Then shall two be in the field; the one shall be taken, and the other left. 41 Two women shall be grinding at the mill; the one shall be taken, and the other left. 42 Watch therefore: for ye know not what hour your Lord doth come. 43 But know this that if the goodman of the house had known in what watch the thief would come, he would have watched, and would not have suffered his house to be broken up. **<u>44 Therefore be ye also ready:</u>** for in such an hour as ye think not the Son of man cometh.

Faithful and wise servant
Matt 24:45 Who then is a faithful and wise servant, whom his lord hath made ruler over his household, to give them meat in due season?

LOOKING FOR THE MASTERS COMING

36- 46 Blessed is that servant, whom his lord when he cometh shall find so doing. 47 Verily I say unto you, That he shall make him ruler over all his goods.

NOT LOOKING FOR THE MASTERS COMING

48 But and if that evil servant shall say in his heart, my lord delayeth his coming; 49 and shall begin to smite his fellow servants, and to eat and drink with the drunken;

This servant had no hope. He had no hope because he was not looking for the return of the master. His focus was on the the delay that he may do as he will and not as the master with. We had many people like that. Rather than to focus on the rapture, they focus on the tribulation. Rather than to look at the object of hope, they look at the object of fear.

THE BLESSED HOPE

Titus 2:12-13 (KJV) Teaching us that, denying ungodliness and worldly lusts, we should live soberly, righteously, and godly, in this present world; **13 Looking for that blessed hope, and the glorious appearing of the great God and our Savior Jesus Christ;**

Noah's blessed hope was the Ark. God told him the flood was coming, and just as I'm warning you Noah warned all the people, and told them a terrible day is coming, and I'm offering you salvation. It is very important that we offer people salvation and let them know that there's a tribulation coming, but they don't have to be left behind.

UNEXPECTED RETURN / EVIL SERVANT

50 The lord of that servant shall come in a day when he looketh not for him, and in an hour that he is not aware of, 51 And shall cut him

asunder, and appoint him his portion with the hypocrites: there shall be weeping and gnashing of teeth.

Notice this was an evil servant, but he was a servant.
Matthew 25 tells of 10 virgins. They were all virgins.
This says we had all Christians some serve in the evil way, some serve in a faithful way. Some versions of foolish, and some virgins or wise. But you may have noticed, all of the virgins did not become the bride, and all of the servants were not rewarded.

WE MUST HAVE A HOPE

1 John 3:1-3 (KJV) Beloved, now are we the sons of God and it doth not yet appear what we shall be: but we know that, when he shall appear, we shall be like him; for we shall see him as he is. **3 And every man that hath this hope in him purifieth himself, even as he is pure.**

REMEMBER / TO WATCH AND PRAY THAT WE MAY ESCAPE

Luke 21:36 (KJV) **Watch ye therefore, and pray always, that ye may be accounted worthy to escape** all these things that shall come to pass, and to stand before the Son of man

REMEMBER / TO BE CAUGHT UP, IS TO ESCAPE

1 Thess 4:16-18 (KJV) 15 For this we say unto you by the word of the Lord, that we which are alive and remain unto the coming of the Lord shall not prevent them which are asleep. 16 For the Lord himself shall descend from heaven with a shout, with the voice of the archangel, and with the trump of God: and the dead in Christ shall rise first: 17 Then we which are alive and remain shall be caught up together with them in the clouds, to meet the Lord in the air: and so shall we ever be with the Lord. 18 Wherefore comfort one another with these words.

REMEMBER WE WILL BE CHANGED

We go also from death to life, from mortality to immortality, from corruption to incorruption

REJOICE

We shall receive a glorified body. Jesus shall change our vile body to be like his. And we cannot yet comprehend this but we know it's good because we shall be like him, and if we love him we rejoice.

DO YOU NEED PRAYER?

Are you going through relationship problems?
Are you depressed?
Do you need healing?
Are you unsure of your salvation?
Are you unsure if there's a heaven or hell?

Let me pray with you a prayer that is guaranteed for God to hear you.

PLEASE PRAY THIS PRAYER FROM YOUR HEART

Dear heavenly father I come before you a sinner.

I believe you sent your son to the earth to live for me, and to die for me, and raised from the dead for me, so that I can experience eternal life, and not hell. Thank you for bearing my sins, so that I don't have to. Come into my heart, and live through me, so that I may live for you. Thank you Lord for saving me.

If you prayed this prayer in faith, please direct correspondence to:

Heaven bound ministries
James H. Rayner
PO Box #235
6425 LEORNARDTOWN RD
BRYANTOWN, MD. 20617

Reflection

ABOUT THE AUTHOR

James H Rayner attended National Bible College in Washington D.C. for Ministerial Intern Training under Dr. TL Lowry.

He then attended Rhema Bible Training Center in Tulsa Oklahoma under Kenneth E. Hagin while working for Oral Roberts at Oral Roberts University as a prayer room counselor.

He then attended Grace Fellowships, School of the Local Church where he focused on the Greek New Testament under Dr. Bob Yandian while working in the counseling department as a counselor. He worked as an addiction and substance abuse counselor, and a depression and suicide prevention counselor.

After pastoring for 10 years in Virginia he was then asked to cohost a radio show in Macon Georgia. With **BB & G Network.** The radio program is called Promises.

Any corespondence can be sent to:
James H. Rayner
PO Box #235
6425 LEORNARDTOWN RD
BRYANTOWN, MD. 20617

Printed in the United States
By Bookmasters